Math Learning Centers
for the Primary Grades

Carole Cook
illustrated by Janet B. Holloman

The Center for Applied
Research in Education, Inc.

West Nyack, New York

Library of Congress Cataloging-in-Publication Data

Cook, Carole
    Math learning centers for the primary grades/Carole Cook;
illustrated by Janet B. Holloman.
      p. cm.
   ISBN 0-87628-574-4
   1. Mathematics—Study and teaching (Primary) I. Title.
   QA135.5.C5953 1992
   372.7—dc20   91–20110
                                          CIP

ISBN 0-87628-574-4

The Center for Applied
Research in Education
Business Information Publishing Division
A division of Simon & Schuster
West Nyack, New York 10995

Printed in the United States of America

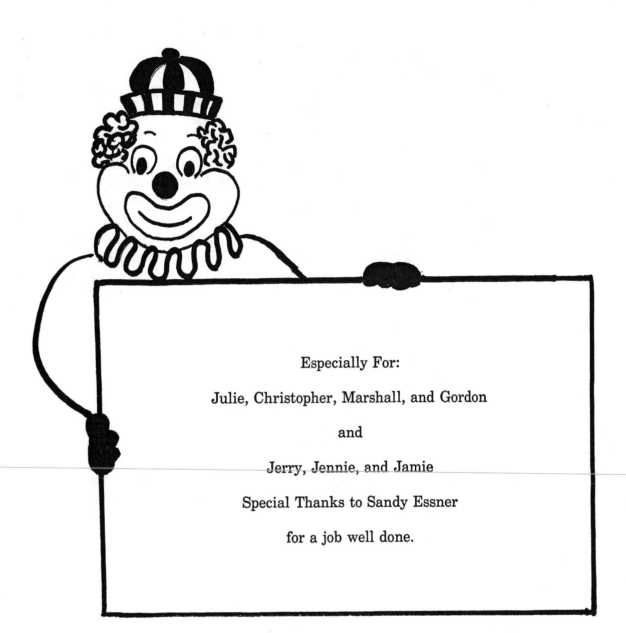

Especially For:

Julie, Christopher, Marshall, and Gordon

and

Jerry, Jennie, and Jamie

Special Thanks to Sandy Essner

for a job well done.

About The Author

Carole Cook has a B.S. and an M.A. from Appalachian State University (Boone, North Carolina) and has taught first grade in Maryland and Virginia for 23 years.

She co-authored *Classroom Nursery Rhymes Activities Kit* (The Center, 1983), *Challenges for Children* (The Center, 1984), *Hands on Geography—Virginia* (Nystrom, 1985), *Practical Activities for Practically Everything* (Fearon Teacher Aids, Simon & Schuster Supplementary Education Group, 1990), and contributed to *The Primary Teacher's Ready-to-Use Activities Program* published by The Center.

About The Illustrator

Janet B. Holloman has been illustrating for the past 20 years, the last five professionally with her own business. For the past 13 years, she has illustrated for teachers and, since 1980, has been a teaching assistant in Prince William County, Virginia.

About This Book

Math Learning Centers for the Primary Grades provides 80 stimulating and manipulative activities for children in grades K-2 and for children with special needs. With these center activities, children are easily motivated and skills are reinforced and extended. Since children require a variety of techniques and opportunities to practice a skill, math learning centers can meet their needs and provide enjoyment at the same time. Research has shown that going from the concrete to the semiconcrete to the abstract has proven to be the most effective way of acquiring a true understanding of math, so manipulatives are a very important part of these centers.

Math learning centers are intended to be a supplement to the regular math program and are not to be used in its place. Activities are developed around skills and concepts needed by primary students to establish a basic foundation in mathematics. The centers may be used with any teaching and classroom management system. However, an easy-to-use record keeping and maintenance system is included for your convenience.

Math Learning Centers for the Primary Grades offers the following ten units:

- Numbers to 20
- Addition to 10
- Subtraction to 10
- Place value
- Telling time
- Money
- Measurement
- Geometry
- Fractions
- Addition and subtraction to 19

Within each unit are activities with varying levels of difficulty specifically designed to meet the wide range of needs in the primary classroom. Each math learning center has a ready-to-use reproducible student activity sheet to assist you in keeping track of student progress. A variety of easily available and free materials is used in construction of the centers from beans and macaroni to butter tubs and coffee cans to berry baskets, toothpicks, and styrofoam packing pieces. Illustrations are provided to help you construct the centers and assist in their development.

With *Math Learning Centers for the Primary Grades,* you can make learning centers an important part of your teaching program to help develop independent learners. The materials offered here will guide you in reaching that goal.

Carole Cook

To The Teacher

The ten units in *Math Learning Centers for the Primary Grades* are given in sequential order. However, some units—such as for fractions, telling time, and measurement—may be used at any time.

Features of Each Unit

Each unit contains between 7 and 13 centers, including a graphing problem-solving activity and a triple-star challenger. Each center has a stated objective, a list of materials needed, a procedure to follow for making the center, directions to the student, and a student activity sheet. Illustrations are provided to make the construction easier for you.

A student activity sheet is ready to be reproduced for recording student work at the center. For some centers, a Teacher Time Saver is also provided to assist you in making the center with ease.

A triple-star activity is included near the end of each unit. The triple star is a think-and-make activity that gives each child the opportunity to do a challenging math activity using all the skills learned in the unit or to make an object related to the unit to take home.

The graphing problem-solving centers allow students to make and/or interpret graphs that are related to the particular unit. Some of the graphing is done by individual students while others require students to work together in a cooperative learning situation.

Most activities contain information about correlation with other content areas. These are labeled "Content Hints."

Special Feature

At the end of this book is a set of instant Monthly Math Centers. It is quick to reproduce, can be sent home for a parent helper to color and cut out, and requires only a plastic sandwich bag to be ready to use. Since the pieces are programmed by you, the centers can be used at any grade level and can be any level of difficulty.

Record Keeping

Since you may want to keep a close check on student progress in the math centers, a simple management system is provided.

You should provide a folder for each child to store completed center work. Staple the assignment sheet on the inside of the folder, as shown in the illustration. If you wish the student to do only certain centers in a unit, circle the numbers of the centers he or she is to complete. The student puts a check mark on the assignment sheet when he or she is finished with a center and puts the student activity sheet in the folder. You evaluate the completed sheet and also put a check mark if the work is satisfactory. If the student has had difficulty, you can write the words "see me" in the space.

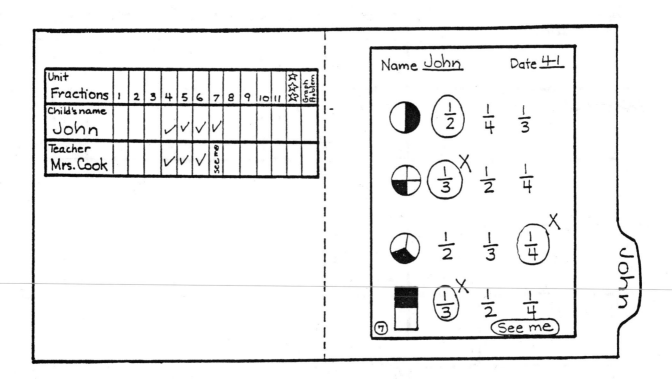

Assigning certain centers to students who have learning disabilities, are slow workers, need reinforcement, or are gifted will provide an approach that meets individual needs.

Record Keeping

Unit		1	2	3	4	5	6	7	8	9	10	11	☆☆☆	Graph Problem
Child's name														
Teacher														

Unit		1	2	3	4	5	6	7	8	9	10	11	☆☆☆	Graph Problem
Child's name														
Teacher														

Unit		1	2	3	4	5	6	7	8	9	10	11	☆☆☆	Graph Problem
Child's name														
Teacher														

Contents

About This Book, v
To the Teacher, vi

Unit 1   Numbers 1 to 20, 1

Pick and Paste (*counting*), 2
   Student Activity Sheet I, 3
   Student Activity Sheet II, 4
Count and Wear (*counting*), 5
   Student Activity Sheet, 6
Stamp It! (*counting*), 7
   Student Activity Sheet I, 8
   Student Activity Sheet II, 9
Made to Order (*ordering numbers*), 10
   Student Activity Sheet, 11
In the Bag (*counting and recording*), 12
   Student Activity Sheet, 13
It's a Match (*number words*), 14
   Student Activity Sheet, 15
Spell and Draw (*number words*), 16
   Student Activity Sheet, 17
   Teacher Time Saver, 18

Bug Me (*number words*), 19
   Student Activity Sheet, 20
Save My Place (*ordinal numbers*), 21
   Student Activity Sheet, 22
   Teacher Time Saver, 23
Twiggles (*ordinal directions*), 24
   Student Activity Sheet I, 25
   Student Activity Sheet II, 26
Pick Two (*greater than/lesser than*), 27
   Student Activity Sheet, 28
Four Square*** (*number problems*), 29
   Teacher Time Saver, 30
Yummy Fruits and Veggies (*graphing*), 31
   Student Activity Sheet, 32

Unit 2   Addition to 10, 33

Clip It (*matching numerals to objects*), 34
   Student Activity Sheet, 35
Thumb Print Critters (*number problems*), 36
   Student Activity Sheet, 37
Magazine Mania (*number problems*), 38
   Teacher Time Saver, 39
Pasta Pickles (*number problems*), 40
   Teacher Time Saver I, 41
   Teacher Time Saver II, 42
Marshmallow Snowman (*number combinations*), 43

   Open-ended Activity Sheet, 44
Amigos (*finding missing addends*), 45
   Student Activity Sheet, 46
Read and Make (*word problems*), 47
   Teacher Time Saver, 48
Indian Hats*** (*adding*), 49
   Teacher Time Saver, 50
All in the Family (*graphing*), 51
   Student Activity Sheet, 52

Unit 3   Subtraction to 10, 53

Put Them to Bed (*subtracting*), 54
   Student Activity Sheet, 55
Food for Thought (*subtracting*), 56
   Student Activity Sheet, 57
One Lump or Two or Three (*subtracting*), 58
   Student Activity Sheet, 59
   Teacher Time Saver, 60
Punch That Ticket (*number problems*), 61
   Student Activity Sheet, 62

Porcupine Quills (*number problems*), 63
   Student Activity Sheet, 64
Gone Fishing (*word problems*), 65
   Student Activity Sheet, 66
   Teacher Time Saver, 67
Zap Those Bugs*** (*subtracting*), 68
   Teacher Time Saver, 69
The Cookie Chef (*graphing*), 70
   Student Activity Sheet, 71

Unit 4   Place Value, 73

Bean-O (*sets of tens/remaining ones*), 74
   Student Activity Sheet, 75
Stringing Tens (*sets of tens*), 76
   Student Activity Sheet, 77
Buttons Buttons (*sets of tens and ones*), 78
   Student Activity Sheet, 79
Train Ride (*place value number problems*), 80
   Student Activity Sheet, 81

Bundle Up (*sets of tens and hundreds*), 82
   Student Activity Sheet, 83
   Teacher Time Saver, 84
Hat Tricks*** (*place value number problems*), 85
Gumdrop Fun (*graphing*), 87
   Student Activity Sheet, 88

Unit 5   Telling Time, 89

Tick-Tock-Clock (*making clock faces*), 90
   Teacher Time Saver, 91
My Time (*times of day*), 92
   Student Activity Sheet, 93
   Teacher Time Saver, 94
Clock Puzzles (*specific times on clock faces*), 95
   Student Activity Sheet, 96
   Teacher Time Saver, 97

Cuddly Clocks (*time word problems*), 98
   Student Activity Sheet, 99
   Teacher Time Saver, 100
Time's Up!*** (*completing tasks in given time*), 101
   Student Activity Sheet, 102
Sweet Dreams (*graphing*), 103
   Student Activity Sheet, 104

Unit 6   Money, 105

Pennies Please (*money less than 10¢*), 106
   Student Activity Sheet, 107
Something Fishy (*nickel money problems to 50¢*), 108
   Student Activity Sheet, 109
   Teacher Time Saver, 110
Ice Cream Shop (*money number problems*), 111
   Student Activity Sheet, 112
Basket of Eggs (*money word problems to 99¢*), 113
   Student Activity Sheet, 114

Shopping Basket (*computing costs/making change*), 115
   Student Activity Sheet, 116
Piggy Banks*** (*saving money*), 117
   Teacher Time Saver, 118
Change Purses (*counting/recording money to 99¢*), 119
   Student Activity Sheet, 120
Allowance Day (*graphing*), 121
   Student Activity Sheet, 122

Unit 7   Measurement, 123

Cheerio! (*measuring in centimeters*), 124
  Student Activity Sheet, 125
Hot, Warm, or Cold (*measuring temperatures*), 126
  Student Activity Sheet, 127
Elf's Rice (*measuring volume*), 128
  Student Activity Sheet, 129
High Flier (*measuring/following directions*), 130

Teacher Time Saver, 131
So Big! (*measuring body parts in centimeters*), 133
  Student Activity Sheet, 134
Play Dough*** (*measuring/following directions*), 135
  Teacher Time Saver, 136
Step on the Scales (*graphing*), 137
  Student Activity Sheet, 138

Unit 8   Geometry, 139

Rice Is Nice! (*geometric terms—polygon, diagonals, line segments*), 140
  Student Activity Sheet I, 141
  Student Activity Sheet II, 142
  Student Activity Sheet III, 143
Feed the Birds (*making geometric shapes*), 144
  Teacher Time Saver, 145
Pizzazz Pizza (*cutting out geometric shapes*), 146
  Student Activity Sheet, 147
  Teacher Time Saver, 148

Geometric Collage (*making a collage*), 149
  Teacher Time Saver I, 150
  Teacher Time Saver II, 151
Salty Shapes (*making geometric shapes*), 152
  Teacher Time Saver, 153
Melvin or Millie Monster!*** (*creating a geometric picture*), 154
  Teacher Time Saver, 155
Shapely Graph (*graphing*), 156
  Student Activity Sheet, 157
  Teacher Time Saver, 158

Unit 9   Fractions, 159

Seasonal Symmetry (*using the term "symmetrical"*), 160
  Student Activity Sheet, 161
  Teacher Time Saver, 162
½ of a Whole Is ½ (*using the fraction ½*), 163
  Student Activity Sheet, 164
  Teacher Time Saver, 165
Sparkling Thirds Mobile (*making a mobile*), 166
  Teacher Time Saver, 167
Spill and Draw (*dividing sets into halves, thirds, fourths*), 168
  Student Activity Sheet, 169

Joe's Grill (*whole/fractional parts*), 170
  Student Activity Sheet, 171
Colored Rice (*measuring/recording amount in cup*), 172
  Student Activity Sheet, 173
Spin a Fraction (*recognizing/reproducing fractions*), 174
  Student Activity Sheet, 175
  Teacher Time Saver, 176
Add a Bead*** (*using the fraction ⅓*), 177
A Tisket, A Tasket Graph (*graphing*), 178
  Student Activity Sheet, 179
  Teacher Time Saver, 180

Unit 10   Addition and Subtraction to 19, 181

Bunny Hop (*subtracting from 19 or less*), 182
  Student Activity Sheet, 183
How Old Are You? (*adding/subtracting*), 184
  Student Activity Sheet, 185
  Teacher Time Saver, 186
Toss and Record (*subtracting from 19 or less*), 187
  Student Activity Sheet, 188
High Rollers (*subtraction number problems*), 189
  Student Activity Sheet, 190

Fruits and Veggies (*subtraction number problems*), 191
  Teacher Time Saver I, 192
  Teacher Time Saver II, 193
Monster Munch (*adding/subtracting to 19*), 194
  Student Activity Sheet, 195
  Teacher Time Saver, 196
Caterwiggle*** (*subtraction facts*), 197
  Teacher Time Saver, 198
Lost Teeth (*graphing*), 199
  Student Activity Sheet, 200

Instant Monthly Math Centers, 201

How to Use, 202
  September, 203
  October, 204
  November, 205
  December, 206

January, 207
February, 208
March, 209
April, 210
May/June, 211

Numbers 1 to 20

PICK AND PASTE

OBJECTIVE: Students will be able to choose numerals and match the numeral with the correct corresponding number of objects.

MATERIALS: 2 plastic berry baskets

macaroni (your choice of shapes)

cards with numerals (activity sheets I and II)

glue

PROCEDURE: 1. Label two berry baskets | macaroni | and | number strips |

2. Put any kind of macaroni noodles into one basket that has been lined with clear wrap, construction paper, or cloth to keep noodles from falling through the cracks.

3. Reproduce the center activity sheets onto colored construction paper and cut apart. Put these strips into the numbers basket.

TEACHER DIRECTIONS TO STUDENTS:

1. Choose 5 different number strips.

2. Read the number and glue on that amount of macaroni.

3. Put your name or initials on each strip and let the macaroni dry.

The macaroni strips may be saved for a math counting activity where each child takes five randomly selected strips and counts the macaroni to make sure the number is correct on the strip. Then the strips are given to the child whose name is on the strip so that he can take his product home.

Pick and Paste

1	2
3	4
5	6
7	8
9	10

Student Activity Sheet I

Pick and Paste

11	12
13	14
15	16
17	18
19	20

COUNT AND WEAR

OBJECTIVE: Students will be able to count objects to ten (or higher as directed by the teacher).

MATERIALS: Strips of yarn 18″ in length—one end should have been dipped in glue and let dry
4 decorated coffee cans for storage
Large macaroni or manicotti
Magic markers
Numerals or number words written on folded pieces of paper
Student activity sheet

PROCEDURE:
1. Dip 18″ pieces of yarn into glue and hang to dry overnight. (This makes it easy for the child to thread the yarn through noodles.)
2. Put large macaroni or manicotti in a decorated and labeled coffee can.
3. Provide magic markers in another labeled coffee can.
4. Put numerals or number words on folded pieces of paper in a fourth coffee can.

TEACHER DIRECTIONS TO STUDENTS:
1. Choose a slip of paper from the can.
2. Use the markers to decorate the same number of macaroni noodles.
3. String them on the yarn and tie a knot to form a necklace.
4. Draw and color your noodles onto the student activity sheet.
5. Show your necklace and the slip of paper to your teacher.

CONTENT HINT: *Social Studies*

Use with unit about Indians on Thanksgiving.

Count and Wear

© 1992 by The Center for Applied Research in Education, Inc.

Student Activity Sheet

STAMP IT!

OBJECTIVE: Students will be able to read a numeral and stamp that number of stamps.

MATERIALS: Stamp pad (of several different colors)
Stamp (a variety of stamps is more interesting)
Student activity sheet
Open activity sheet

PROCEDURE:
1. Put stamps and stamp pads on a table or desk.
2. Reproduce student activity page.

TEACHER DIRECTIONS TO STUDENTS:
1. Read the numeral.
2. Stamp the same number of pictures onto the activity page.

CONTENT HINT: *Social Studies*
Use holiday stamps and colors.
Science
Use animal stamps.

Name _____   Date _____

Stamp It

9	
3	
6	
2	
5	
4	

Student Activity Sheet

Name _____   **Date** _____

Stamp It

MADE TO ORDER

OBJECTIVE: Students will be able to match tactile numerals to objects and put them in ascending order.

MATERIALS: Manilla or colored 9″ × 12″ envelope for storing materials

(10) pieces 3″ × 3″ colored construction paper

Glue

Salt

(10) pieces 3″ × 6″ construction paper

Geometrical shapes

Student activity sheet

PROCEDURE:
1. Cut construction paper into ten 3″ × 3″ pieces.
2. Write numerals desired with glue (1–10), (10–20), (5–15), etc.
3. Sprinkle liberally with salt and let dry.
4. Cut ten 3″ × 6″ pieces of paper.
5. Cut and paste geometric shapes to equal each number on the 3″ × 3″ pieces.

TEACHER DIRECTIONS TO STUDENTS:
1. Match the numeral to the number of objects.
2. Then put them in order from the least to the most.
3. Use the activity sheet to show the matches.

EXAMPLE:

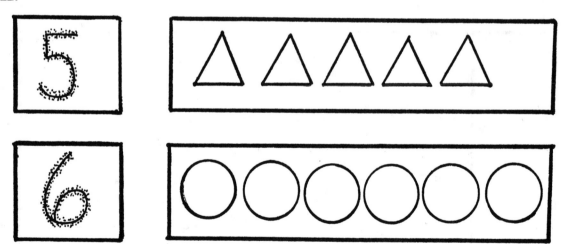

CONTENT HINT: *Social Studies or Science*

Use seasonal stickers or holiday colors for the paper strips.

Name _____ Date _____

Made To Order

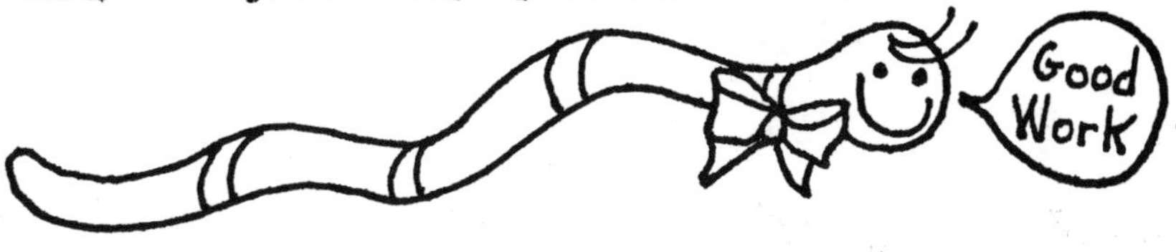

Student Activity Sheet

Good Work

IN THE BAG

OBJECTIVE: Students will be able to count the objects in a bag and record their findings.

MATERIALS: Shoe box, basket, or container to hold all the bags

Clear plastic sandwich bags

Small objects for counting

Masking tape, adhesive tape, blank sticker or self-stick label

Student activity sheet

PROCEDURE:
1. Put labels onto the number of sandwich bags you want in the center (Example: eight bags). Number each bag.

2. Put a different number of objects to be counted in each bag.

TEACHER DIRECTIONS TO STUDENTS:
1. Choose four bags one at a time.
2. Write the bag number on the activity sheet.
3. Count the number of objects in the bag and write the answer.
4. Draw the same number of objects on your activity sheet. They do not have to be the same kind of objects as those in the bag.

CONTENT HINT: Fill the bags with manipulatives to correspond with your science unit of study—Oceans: seashells; Plants: seeds; Geology: rocks. Ask the children for further suggestions.

In The Bag

In bag ☐ there are _____ things.

In bag ☐ there are _____ things.

In bag ☐ there are _____ things.

In bag ☐ there are _____ things.

Student Activity Sheet

IT'S A MATCH!

OBJECTIVE: Students will be able to match number words with the correct amount of objects to form a complete puzzle.

MATERIALS: Large Ziplock bag, box, or can to hold puzzle pieces
Markers, colored pencils, or crayons
Student activity sheet

PROCEDURE: 1. Duplicate student activity sheet onto construction paper or lightweight tag.
2. Draw and color objects to match the number word.
3. Laminate and cut apart puzzle pieces.

 For the tactile learner, use objects such as toasted oat cereal, ball-shaped colored cereal, beans, etc., to show the number word.

TEACHER DIRECTIONS TO STUDENTS: 1. Match up the number word and objects to make a puzzle.
2. On your activity sheet draw the objects that match the word.
3. After they have been checked, cut apart your puzzles. Put them in a bag or envelope to use at home.

It's A Match!

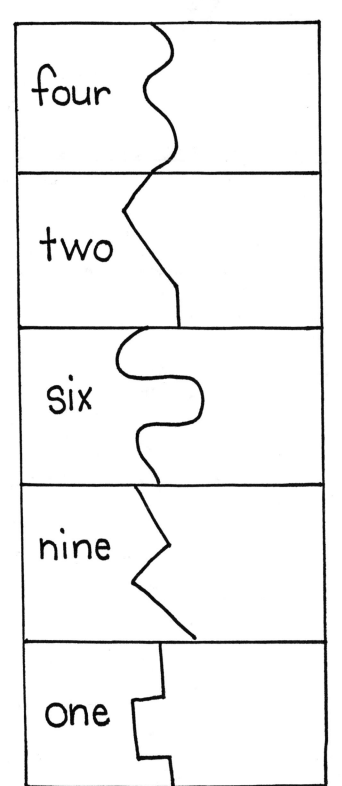
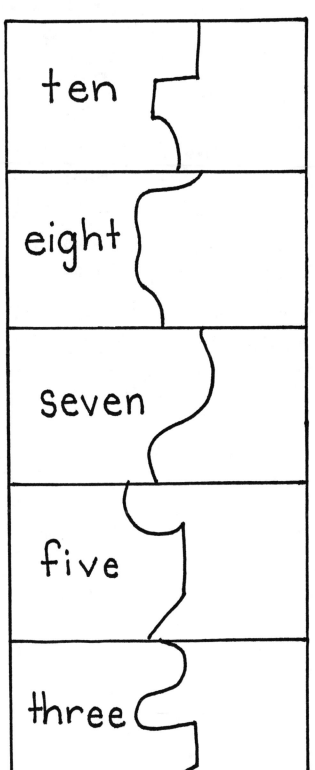

SPELL AND DRAW

OBJECTIVE: Students will be able to read a number word, spell it with magnetic letters, and write it on their paper.

MATERIALS: Magnetic board or surface

Magnetic letters

Ziplock bag

Number words on folded paper

Student activity sheet

Teacher time saver sheet

PROCEDURE:
1. Reproduce number words, cut apart, fold, and put into a Ziplock bag.
2. Place magnetic board and letters on a table.

TEACHER DIRECTIONS TO STUDENTS:
1. Choose four number words from the bag.
2. Using magnetic letters copy the words onto the magnetic board.
3. Now write one word in each box of your activity sheet.
4. Draw the number of objects each word tells you.

CONTENT HINT: *Social Studies and Science*

Ask the children to make seasonal pictures such as pumpkins or ghosts in October, chicks and eggs in April, or birds and flowers in May.

Name _____ **Date** _____

Spell and Draw

Student Activity Sheet

Spell and Draw

one	two
three	four
five	six
seven	eight
nine	ten
eleven	twelve
thirteen	fourteen
fifteen	sixteen
seventeen	eighteen
nineteen	twenty

BUG ME

OBJECTIVE: Students will be able to match number words to corresponding number of objects.

MATERIALS: Bulletin board
Enlarged version of bug
Student activity sheet
Clear self-stick vinyl
Construction paper

PROCEDURE:
1. Enlarge and color the bug from the student activity sheet.
2. Cut out the bug and laminate for long lasting use.
3. Write number words on colored construction paper.
4. Reproduce student activity sheet.
5. Put the bug on a bulletin board in the math center area.

TEACHER DIRECTIONS TO STUDENTS:
1. Pin the number word next to the same number of flowers.
2. On your activity sheet copy the number word next to the same amount of flowers.

CONTENT HINT: *Science*

Useful activity for plant unit. Don't forget to discuss how we care for plants by keeping pests away.

Bug Me

Student Activity Sheet

SAVE MY PLACE

OBJECTIVE: Students will be able to place ordinal numbers in sequence from first to tenth.

MATERIALS: Bulletin board
Flowers from Teacher Time Saver sheet
Construction paper
Colored markers
Student activity sheet
Scissors and glue
Clear self-stick vinyl

PROCEDURE:
1. Reproduce ten buggy flowers and circles on construction paper.
2. Color with markers and write an ordinal number on each separate circle.
3. Cut out and laminate.
4. Arrange flowers on a bulletin board.
5. Put ordinal numbered circles into a bag pinned to the bulletin board.

TEACHER DIRECTIONS TO STUDENTS:
1. Using thumbtacks or pushpins match the number word to the correct flower and bug.
2. On your activity sheet cut out the number word and paste it on the correct flower in the row.
3. You may color your flowers and bugs if you wish.

CONTENT HINT: *Science*

Working on Plants or a unit on Spring would be a great time to use this center.

Instead of using flowers on the board, why not use pumpkins for Halloween or Christmas trees for Christmas.

Save My Place

Name _____

Date _____

fifth

tenth

second

seventh

fourth

first

eighth

third

sixth

ninth

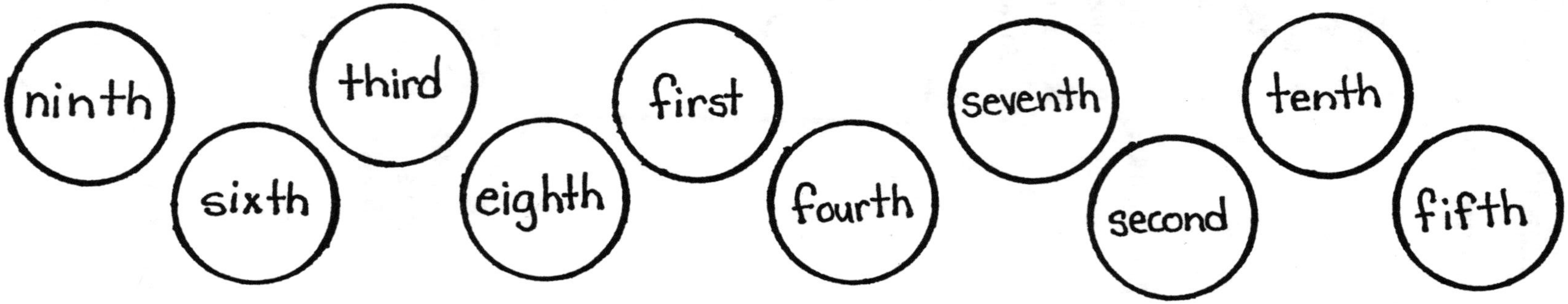

Student Activity Sheet

Save My Place

Teacher Time Saver

TWIGGLES

OBJECTIVE: Students will be able to follow ordinal directions.

MATERIALS: Toothpicks or long fruit skewers
Tempera or spray paint
Styrofoam packing pieces
Five berry baskets
Clay
Plastic bag
Student activity sheet I (easy)
Student activity sheet II (hard)

PROCEDURE:
1. Spray paint the styrofoam pieces (or paint with tempera) using five different colors of paint: red, blue, green, yellow and orange.
2. Put the styrofoam pieces into the berry baskets according to color.
3. Toothpicks or skewers can stay in the box they come in.
4. Small amounts of clay to hold the toothpick creation upright.
5. Student activity sheet reproduced, cut apart, and placed in a plastic bag.

   *NOTE: Teacher chooses easy or harder parts of the activity sheet according to grade or math level of the student.

TEACHER DIRECTIONS TO STUDENTS:
1. Choose a piece of paper from the bag.
2. Read the directions to make your Twiggle.
3. Stand your Twiggle in a small amount of clay on the paper you chose.
4. Don't forget to put your name on the paper.

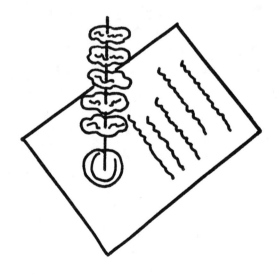

Twiggles I

Name _____

Put on green—first
    yellow—second
    blue—third
    red—fourth
    orange—fifth

Name _____

Put on red—first
    blue—second
    orange—third
    yellow—fourth
    green—fifth

Name _____

Put on blue—first
    green—second
    red—third
    orange—fourth
    yellow—fifth

Name _____

Put on blue—first
    orange—second
    yellow—third
    green—fourth
    red—fifth

Name _____

Put on orange—first
    red—second
    green—third
    blue—fourth
    yellow—fifth

Name _____

Put on yellow—first
    green—second
    red—third
    orange—fourth
    blue—fifth

Student Activity Sheet

Twiggles II

Name _____

Put on 2 red—first
3 yellow—second
1 blue—third
3 orange—fourth
2 green—fifth

(clay) What color is the nineth from the bottom? _____

Name _____

Put on 3 green—first
1 red—second
4 yellow—third
2 blue—fourth
1 orange—fifth

(clay) What color is the sixth from the top? _____

Name _____

Put on 4 yellow—first
1 orange—second
3 blue—third
1 green—fourth
2 red—fifth

(clay) What color is the eleventh from the bottom? _____

Name _____

Put on 2 orange—first
3 blue—second
1 red—third
4 yellow—fourth
4 green—fifth

(clay) What color is the thirteen from the top? _____

Name _____

Put on 3 blue—first
4 red—second
2 green—third
1 orange—fourth
5 yellow—fifth

What color is the fourteenth from the top? _____

(clay)

Name _____

Put on 4 green—first
3 yellow—second
3 orange—third
2 blue—fourth
4 red—fifth

What color is the fifteenth from the bottom? _____

(clay)

© 1992 by The Center for Applied Research in Education, Inc.

Student Activity Sheet

Good work

PICK TWO

OBJECTIVE: Students will be able to count two sets of objects and determine which is greater or less.

MATERIALS: 10 film containers

Two or more different kinds of beans or small macaroni

Student activity sheet

Red and blue crayon

Pencil

PROCEDURE:
1. Label, number, and fiill 10 empty film containers with varying numbers of beans or macaroni.
2. Provide reproducible student activity sheet.
   Ex:

TEACHER DIRECTIONS TO STUDENTS:
1. Pick two containers and spill out the contents.
2. Count each set.
3. Draw each set on the activity page.
4. Put a red circle around the set with the greater amount.
5. Put a blue circle around the set with less.
6. Replace the contents in the containers.
7. Now pick two more cans and do it again!

CONTENT HINT: *Science*

For ecology unit, use bottle caps and styrofoam pieces.

Holiday candies are great for Halloween, Christmas, Valentines Day, and Easter.

Sea shells are useful for an ocean unit.

Pick Two

Draw the objects in the container and write the can number. Put a red circle around the greater set and a blue circle around the set with less.

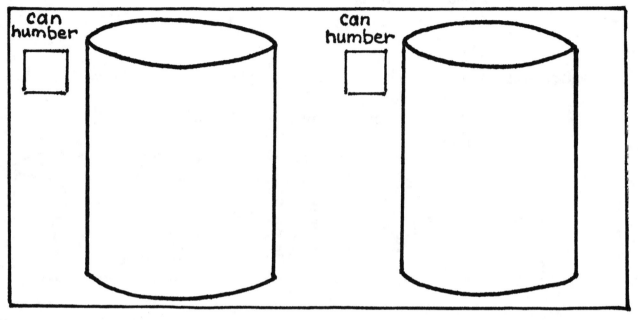

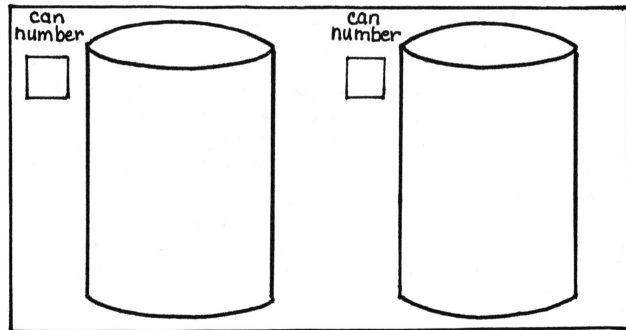

This is fun!

FOUR SQUARE

OBJECTIVE: Students will be able to read number problems and follow directions.

MATERIALS: Cheerios™
Glue
Two large butter tubs
Teacher Time Saver
9″ × 12″ newsprint or manila

PROCEDURE:
1. Fill one large butter tub with Cheerios™.
2. Reproduce several of the Teacher time saver sheets and cut apart. Fold each strip of paper and put in the other butter tub.
3. Put a Triple Star (☆ ☆ ☆) sign on the tubs.
4. Provide 9″ × 12″ paper.

TEACHER DIRECTIONS TO STUDENTS:
1. Fold your paper in half two times and open it up flat.
2. Select four strips of paper from the tub.
3. Glue one strip in each of the four boxes on the paper.
4. Read the directions on the strip of paper and show your answer using Cheerios™ glued to the square.

Ex.

Four Square

2 more than 3	3 less than 7
comes between 11 and 13	comes after 18
six less than fourteen	five more than five
6 + 3 - 7 + 2 - 3	thirteen less than sixteen
1 more than 3 less 2	comes between 10 and 15 (you choose the number)
comes after fifteen	10 - 3 - 4 + 6 - 1 + 10
half of six	half of eight
4 less than 7 + 2	5 more than 8 - 1

YUMMY FRUITS AND VEGGIES

OBJECTIVE: Students will be able to make a graph using a given number of objects.

MATERIALS: Four kinds of plastic fruit or vegetables

Crayons, markers, or colored pencils

Student activity sheet, floor graphing mat

PROCEDURE:
1. Draw the four types of fruit and vegetables you are providing in the boxes at the bottom of the graph sheet and duplicate.
2. Duplicate student activity sheet.
3. Put fruit and vegetables in a large bowl or basket.
4. Provide crayons for recording results.

TEACHER DIRECTIONS TO STUDENTS:
1. Arrange your fruits and vegetables into like groups.
2. Then put each group into a line on a floor graphing mat.
3. Starting at the bottom of the graph, color in one box for each piece of fruit or vegetable you have.
4. Answer the questions at the bottom of the activity sheet.

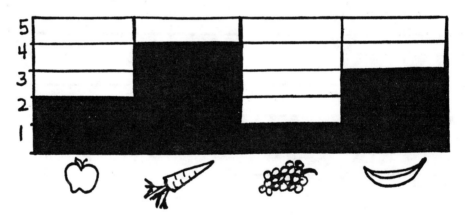

CONTENT HINT: *Health*

Correlates with food and teeth unit.

Social Studies

When studying Fall, Harvest time, or Community Helpers (Grocer) use this activity.

Name _____ Date _____

Yummy Fruits and Veggies

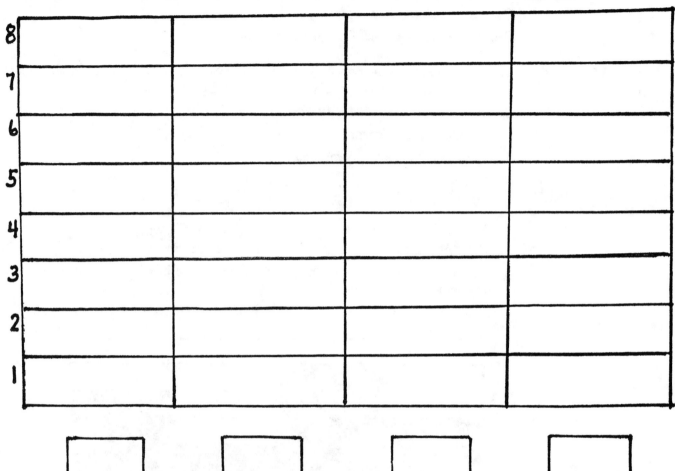

1. How many ⬜ were there? _____
2. Which had more ⬜ or ⬜? _____
3. Which had less ⬜ or ⬜? _____
4. Which do you like best? _____ Why? _____
_____

Addition to 10

CLIP IT

OBJECTIVE: Students will be able to match numerals to the same number of objects.

MATERIALS: Tag or cardboard circle
Clothespins (spring type)
Ziplock bag or clothespins
Student activity sheet

PROCEDURE:
1. Divide the tag or cardboard circle into sections by drawing lines with your marker.
2. Draw and color two sets of objects for each section.
3. With a felt-tip pen write the corresponding numeral onto the clothespin.
4. Students clip clothespins onto the matching section.

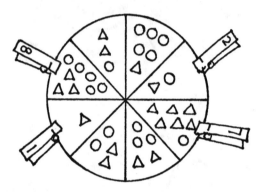

The teacher can also choose to put three-dimentional objects, such as beans, onto each section for the tactile learner.

TEACHER DIRECTIONS TO STUDENTS
1. Clip the clothespins onto the correct number of objects.
2. Make your answer sheet look just like the circle by drawing with markers, crayons, or colored pencils.

CONTENT HINT: *Science and Social Studies*

Use plant, animal, or holiday stickers on the wheel.

Name _____ Date _____

Clip It

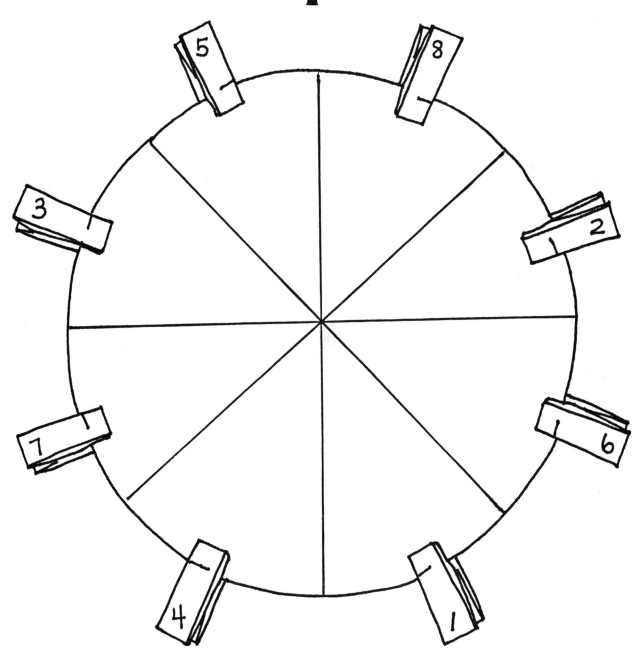

Student Activity Sheet

THUMB PRINT CRITTERS

OBJECTIVE: Students will create addition number stories using thumb prints and write the numerals to show the number story.

MATERIALS: Ink pads

Fine line markers or pencils

Student activity sheet

PROCEDURE:
1. Put several ink pads on the work space.
2. Put fine line markers, pencils, or colored pencils in a can or box.
3. Duplicate the student activity sheet.

TEACHER DIRECTIONS TO STUDENTS:
1. On your worksheet make some thumb prints that total the number in the box.
2. Put in a + sign to show what you are adding.
3. Write the numerals to show the number story as in number 6 on the worksheet.
4. Decorate your "critters" with the markers or pencils.

*The teacher will need to discuss the various types of "critters" you can make with the thumb prints: rabbits, jack-o'-lanterns, mice, cats, bees, flowers, etc.

CONTENT HINT: Use with Science unit about animals or plants, or Social Studies unit on holidays.

Name _____   Date _____

Thumb Print Critters

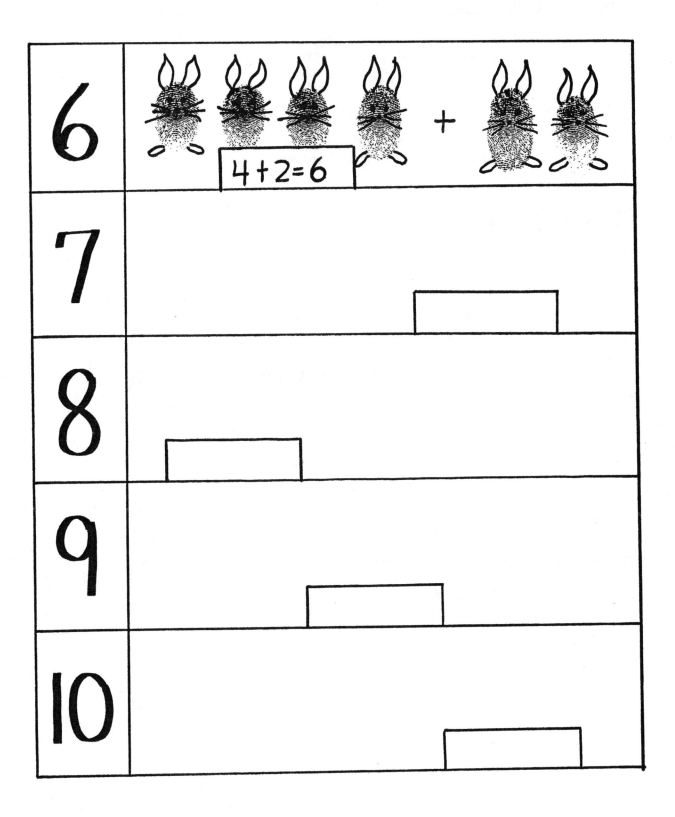

Student Activity Sheet

MAGAZINE MANIA

OBJECTIVE: Using magazine pictures students will create a number problem when the sum is given.

MATERIALS: Magazines

Glue

3″ × 18″ strips of plain newsprint

Time saver activity sheet

PROCEDURE:
1. Provide various magazines with a lot of pictures.
2. Reproduce activity sheet and cut apart.
3. Cut 3″ × 18″ strips of plain newsprint.

TEACHER DIRECTIONS TO STUDENTS:
1. Choose a paper with a sum and a picture.
2. Paste it onto a newsprint strip.
3. Cut out that amount of the shown picture and past onto the strip.
4. You *must* put in the = and + signs to show your number story.

Example:

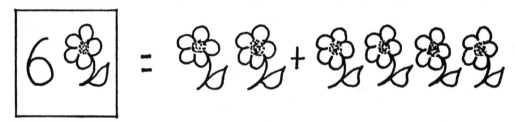

For more advanced students, have them write a word problem on the back of the paper that would reflect their picture story.

CONTENT HINT: For Science units use plant or animal magazines. For Social Studies use magazines with people, cars, or houses. For Health units use magazines devoted to food, exercise equipment, or clothing magazines.

Magazine Mania

5	6	7
8	9	10
5	6	7
8	9	10
8	9	10

Teacher Time Saver

PASTA PICKLES

OBJECTIVE: Students will demonstrate knowledge of addition problems by recreating the problem using two kinds of pasta.

MATERIALS: Two kinds of small pasta

Glue

Two yogurt cups

Two small boxes or containers

Teacher time saver sheets

PROCEDURE:
1. Duplicate "pickle" page onto green construction paper and cut apart on the lines. Place in a small box.
2. Reproduce "problem strip" page and cut apart. Stack face down as in a deck of cards in a small box.
3. Put pasta into two separate containers such as yogurt cups.

  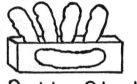 

Pasta   Pasta   Pickle Stack   Addition Strips

TEACHER DIRECTIONS TO STUDENTS:
1. Make four Pasta Pickles—cut on the lines to make pickle shapes.
2. Choose four additional problems from the stack.
3. Paste your addition problem on the plain side of the pickle.
4. Show the number combination by pasting two kinds of pasta on each pickle.

After the pickles are dry, allow children to work in pairs, trade pickles and tell each other the addition facts. Children can check to see if they are correct by looking on the back of the pickle.

CONTENT HINT: Use with a Health unit on food and nutrition or Science unit about plants.

Pasta Pickles

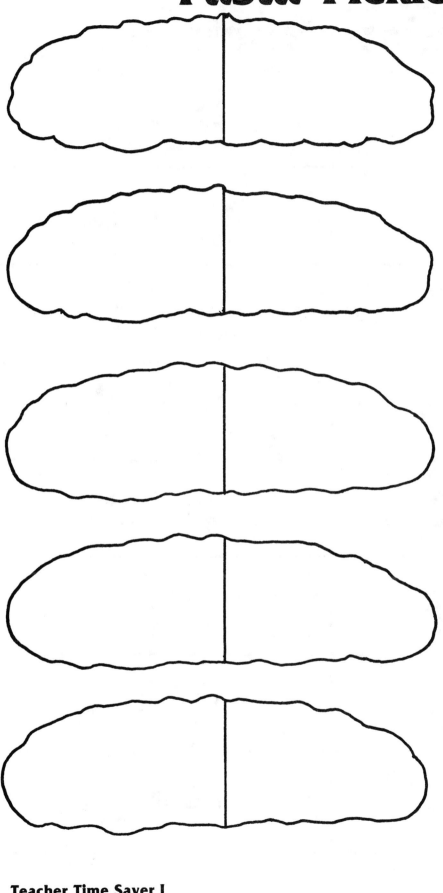
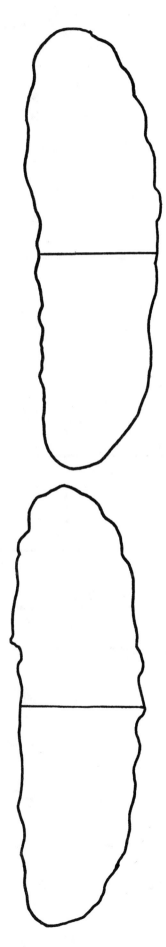

Addition Problems

4 + 3	4 + 6
6 + 1	5 + 4
3 + 2	2 + 8
9 + 1	3 + 3
2 + 7	1 + 5
4 + 4	7 + 3
5 + 3	8 + 2
3 + 6	4 + 0

MARSHMALLOW SNOWMAN

OBJECTIVE: Students will create a marshmallow snowman by using two sizes of marshmallows that total ten or less.

MATERIALS:
One bag large marshmallows
One bag small marshmallows
One box toothpicks
Open-ended student activity sheet
Plastic containers or Ziplock bags

PROCEDURE:
1. Put marshmallows in plastic containers or Ziplock bags to keep them soft.
2. Put toothpicks in a box, can, or easily accessible container.
3. Duplicate student activity sheet.

TEACHER DIRECTIONS TO STUDENTS:
1. Think of number combinations that make ten.
2. Write them on your activity sheet.
3. Circle the one you chose to make your snowman.
4. Put the snowman together using marshmallows and toothpicks.
5. Make a small picture of your snowman using circles to show what it looked like.

CONTENT HINT: Use with Science unit about winter or seasons.

Marshmallow Snowman

Write the number combinations that make 10. Circle the one you chose.

_____

My snowman looked like this.

Open-ended Activity Sheet

AMIGOS

OBJECTIVE: Students will be able to find missing addends by making both sides of an equation the same.

MATERIALS: Small size dried beans in plastic container
Glue
Student activity sheet

PROCEDURE:
1. Put beans in a plastic container for easy access.
2. Reproduce activity sheet.

TEACHER DIRECTIONS TO STUDENTS:
1. Put in the number of beans the numeral says on each tortilla.
2. Then decide how many you need to put in the empty set so that you will have the same amount on both sides.
3. Write the numeral in the box to show how many you put into the empty set.

CONTENT HINT: Correlate with Social Studies unit about Mexico or Health unit about foods.

Amigos

Name _____ Date _____

$$3 + \square = 6$$

$$4 + \square = 9$$

$$2 + \square = 7$$

$$\square + 3 = 8$$

Student Activity Sheet

READ AND MAKE

OBJECTIVE: Students will read a word problem and illustrate the problem.

MATERIALS:

Teacher time saver	Potatoes
Toothpicks	Several kinds of pasta
Construction paper	Foil
Pipe cleaners	Large boxes (cereal type)
Wiggle eyes	Small boxes (jewelry type)
Butter tubs	Cloth scraps
Glue	

PROCEDURE:
1. Reproduce several copies of the time saver, cut apart, and stack face down.
2. Put various materials in containers for each access.

TEACHER DIRECTIONS TO STUDENTS:
1. Choose a paper from the top of the stack.
2. Read the story problem and write the number story in the space.

ex: / $\overline{3+1+2+4=10}$ /

3. Now create the object following the directions.

CONTENT HINT: Follow up with a creative writing lesson about the object the student created.

Read and Make

Name _____

Make a robot with one large box, three pipe cleaners, two little boxes, two strips of paper, and two wiggle eyes. Write the numerals and show the sum.

Name _____

Build a house with two boxes, four pieces of paper, and three pieces of pasta. Write the numerals and show the sum.

Name _____

Make a girl. Use three pieces of cloth, two pieces of construction paper, two wiggle eyes, and one pipe cleaner. Write the addition story.

Name _____

Make a car with one small box, four pieces of round pasta, one piece of foil, and two pipe cleaners. Write the addition story.

Name _____

Make a space station. Use one butter tub, five toothpicks, one piece of foil, and three pieces of pasta. Write your story problem using numerals.

Name _____

Make a funny critter. Use two potatoes, four toothpicks, two pieces of pasta, and two pipe cleaners. Write a number problem to show how many objects you used.

Name _____

Make a monster. Use 2 pieces of construction paper, one box, three wiggle eyes, one piece of foil, and three toothpicks. Write a number story to show how many objects you used.

Name _____

Make a "new" kind of plant. Use one potatoe, two pipe cleaners, 3 pieces of construction paper, and four pieces of pasta. Write a number story to show how many objects you used.

INDIAN HATS

OBJECTIVE: Students will demonstrate knowledge of addition by creating an Indian headband.

MATERIALS: Various colors of construction paper

Colored markers

Scissors

Glue

Pattern or feathers

PROCEDURE:
1. Trace patterns for feathers. (Students may make their own feathers without patterns.)
2. Cut colored construction paper into 3″ × 6″ strips.
3. Cut brown construction paper $2\frac{1}{2}$″ × 24″ for headbands.
4. Reproduce and cup apart "Addition Problems" page.

TEACHER DIRECTIONS TO STUDENTS:
1. Choose an addition problem strip.
2. Choose two colors for your feathers.
3. Trace or cut out your own feathers to show the addition fact.
4. Paste the feathers onto the headband.
5. Paste the addition strip to the inside of the headband.
6. Decorate the headband with Indian designs using the markers.
7. The teacher will staple the headband to fit.

Make your own addition strips with addition problems to 10 *but* adding three or four facts.

Example: / $\overline{3+1+2+4}$ / This would make a very colorful headband. Also students create their own math problem adding to 10, write it on a blank strip, and illustrate with feathers.

CONTENT HINT: Use with Social Studies unit on Indians, Thanksgiving, or colonial America.

Feather Patterns

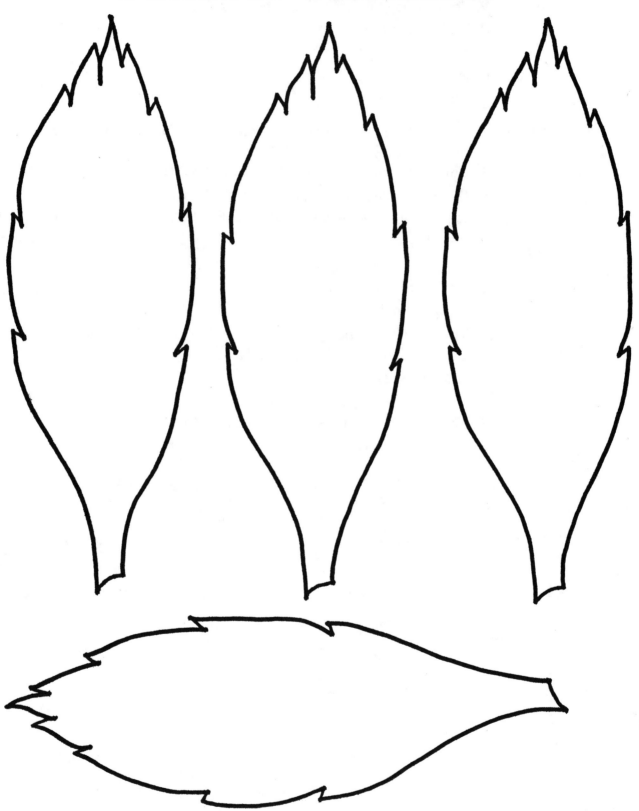

Teacher Time Saver

ALL IN THE FAMILY

OBJECTIVE: Students will be able to record male and female family members living at their house and add the two together to get a total for the male and female column.

MATERIALS: Student activity sheet

Crayons

Pencil

TEACHER DIRECTIONS TO STUDENTS:

1. On your paper color one box for each male or female living at your house.
2. Make sure you start with the bottom box.
3. In the last column color a box for each person living at your house.
4. Answer the questions on your paper.
5. Then go to the large classroom graph and color the same amount of boxes.

   *The teacher would want to make a large graph to accommodate all students in the classroom.

CONTENT HINT: This is a very good activity to use with a Social Studies unit on families since it incorporates all family members living in a household: aunts, grandparents, cousins, etc.

All in the Family

12		
11		
10		
9		
8		
7		
6		
5		
4		
3		
2		
1		

Female   Male   and

How many females live at your house? ____
How many males live at your house? ____
How many people live at your house? ____
Which are there more of? ____
How many more? ____
Fill in the correct spaces on the
   large graph for the classroom.
How many males are on the classroom
   graph? ____
How many females are on the classroom
   graph? ____

Student Activity Sheet

$$\begin{array}{r} 5 \\ -\,1 \\ \hline 4 \end{array}$$

Subtraction to 10

PUT THEM TO BED

OBJECTIVE: Students will subtract from ten or less using non-flexible clothespins.

MATERIALS: Ten non-flexible wooden clothespins

Small piece of material (8″ × 10″ or less)

Shoe box

Magic markers

Tempera paint

Subtraction fact cards

Crayons

Student Activity Sheet and crayons

PROCEDURE:

1. With markers, paint faces on the round part of each clothespin. (Clothing or paint can be added to create finished look for clothespin people.)
2. Turn shoe box upside down and paint it to look like a bed.
3. Cut a small piece of material that would be used as a blanket.
4. Copy and cut apart subtraction fact cards.
5. Copy Student Activity Sheet.

TEACHER DIRECTIONS TO STUDENTS:

1. Turn the stack of cards upside down and take the top card.
2. Start the subtraction problem by putting the clothespin people to bed and covering the ones that go to sleep quickly with the blanket.
3. Count those that are left—they are wide awake!
4. Use your crayons on the Student Activity Sheet to put a blanket over those that go to sleep.
5. Write the answer to show how many are wide awake.

CONTENT HINT: *Health*

Use when working on healthy habits such as getting enough sleep.

Name _____ Date _____

Put Them to Bed

Color a blanket on the clothespin people that go to sleep quickly. Write how many are awake.

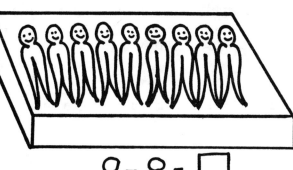

8 - 6 = ☐

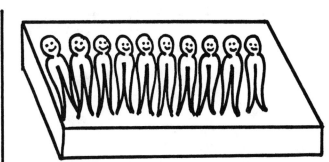

10 - 4 = ☐

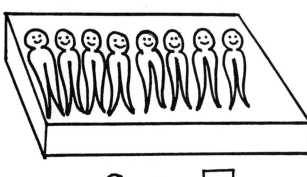

9 - 8 = ☐

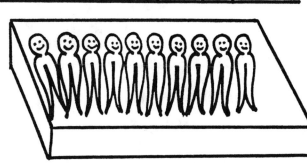

10 - 7 = ☐

8 - 2 = ☐

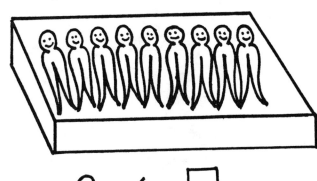

9 - 6 = ☐

Student Activity Sheet

FOOD FOR THOUGHTS

OBJECTIVE: Students will subtract using Cheerios™ or other cereal.

MATERIALS: Small paper plates
Cheerios™
Glue
Student Activity Sheet

PROCEDURE:
1. Write subtraction problems on small paper plates with a magic marker. (Use colorful or decorated paper plates for an attractive center.)
2. Put an ample supply of Cheerios™ in a bowl.
3. Copy the Student Activity Sheet for each student.
4. Supply a bottle of glue.

TEACHER DIRECTIONS TO STUDENTS:
1. Use the Cheerios™ to show the beginning number in the problem on the plate.
2. Remove the ones to be taken away and count those you have left.
3. Practice with each of the plates in the center.
4. Using the Student Activity Sheet, put down the beginning amount of Cheerios™ for each problem. You may eat those you are to take away! Glue those that are left to the plate and write the answer in the box.

CONSTANT HINT: *Health*

Use with a unit on food, nutrition, or to emphasize eating a good breakfast.

Name _____ Date _____

Food for Thought

Put oat cereal on each plate to show the subtraction problem. Eat those you are to take away. Glue on those you have left. Write the answer in the box.

10-3=☐

9-5=☐

7-2=☐

8-7=☐

6-2=☐

7-4=☐

Student Activity Sheet

ONE LUMP OR TWO OR THREE

OBJECTIVE: Students will subtract from ten using sugar cubes.

MATERIALS: Sugar cubes
Plastic cup and saucer
Ice or sugar tongs (optional)
Small plastic dish or plate
Baggies
Student Activity Sheet
Teacher Time Saver sheet

PROCEDURE:
1. Using Baggies, put ten or fewer sugar cubes in as many bags as desired.
2. Write either a 1, 2, or 3 on a small slip of paper and put into each bag.
3. Make a copy of the Student Activity Sheet for each child.
4. Put cup, saucer, and plate in the center.

TEACHER DIRECTIONS TO STUDENTS:
1. Select a Baggie and empty the sugar cubes onto the plate.
2. Count the cubes and write how many there are on the Activity Sheet.
3. Read the number on the slip of paper and put that many cubes into the cup. Then draw that many in the cup on the activity sheet and write it down. Count how many cubes are left and write the answer.

Example:

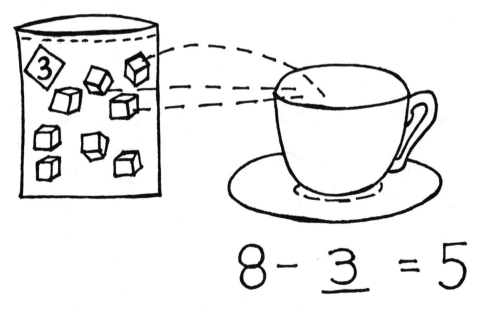

$$8 - \underline{3} = 5$$

One Lump or Two or Three

Write the subtraction problem. Draw the sugar cubes that were used in the cup.

___ − ___ = ___

___ − ___ = ___

___ − ___ = ___

___ − ___ = ___

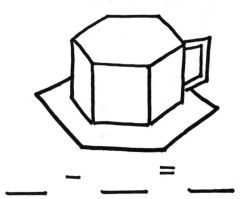

___ − ___ = ___

___ − ___ = ___

Student Activity Sheet

$7 - 3 =$	$5 - 2 =$
$10 - 7 =$	$9 - 9 =$
$8 - 6 =$	$7 - 3 =$
$9 - 8 =$	$10 - 8 =$
$6 - 5 =$	$9 - 4 =$
$10 - 6 =$	$4 - 3 =$
$8 - 7 =$	$7 - 5 =$

Teacher Time Saver

PUNCH THAT TICKET

OBJECTIVE: Students will use manipulatives such as beans to do subtraction problems.

MATERIALS: Beans or other manipulatives
Hole punch
Scissors
Paper clips
Student activity sheet

PROCEDURE:
1. Put a can of beans or other manipulatives at the center for students to do the subtraction problems with.
2. Supply hole punch, scissors, and paper clips.
3. Copy the Student Activity Sheet. (Using colored paper makes the tickets look real.)

TEACHER DIRECTIONS TO STUDENTS:
1. Cut out each ticket on your Student Activity Sheet.
2. Work on the subtraction problem on the ticket using the beans and write the answer in the box.
3. Use the hole punch to punch the number of holes in the ticket to show your answer.
4. Clip tickets together with a paper clip.

CONTENT HINT: *Social Studies*

Use with a unit on transportation or community helpers.

Punch that Ticket

Ticket
9 – 8 = ☐

Ticket
10 – 3 = ☐

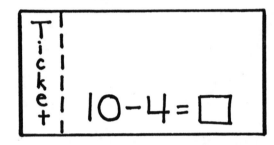

Ticket
8 – 1 = ☐

Ticket
6 – 2 = ☐

Ticket
7 – 4 = ☐

Ticket
5 – 1 = ☐

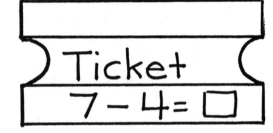

6 – 1 = ☐
Ticket

Ticket
8 – 2 = ☐

PORCUPINE QUILLS

OBJECTIVE: Students will be able to subtract by using toothpicks to solve the problems.

MATERIALS: Clay or playdough
Toothpicks
Student Activity Sheet

PROCEDURE:
1. Put a container of clay or play dough at the center.
2. Provide a box of round toothpicks. (Scrap paper or used computer paper is good to roll clay on—it keeps the area clean.)
3. Copy and cut apart subtraction problems from Teacher Time Saver.
4. Copy Student Activity Sheet for each student.

TEACHER DIRECTIONS TO STUDENTS:
1. With your clay, make a body for a porcupine.
2. Draw a subtraction card from the upside down cards.
3. Put quills (toothpicks) on the porcupine.
4. Remove the amount you are to take away.
5. Think of how many you had left.
6. Do this with all the cards.
7. Using the Student Activity Sheet, draw the quills the porcupine has to start with. Use your black crayon to color the quills he shoots.
8. Write the answer to show how many quills the porcupine has left.

CONTENT HINT: Use with animal unit—how animals protect themselves.

Porcupine Quills

Draw the porcupine quills. Color black the ones that are shot. Write the amount left.

$10 - 3 = \square$

$8 - 6 = \square$

$9 - 3 = \square$

$10 - 7 = \square$

$9 - 4 = \square$

$7 - 1 = \square$

GONE FISHING

OBJECTIVE: Students will read subtraction story problems, record them, and show their answers by gluing on fish-shaped crackers.

MATERIALS: Fish-shaped crackers

Glue

Pencil

Teacher Time Saver

Student Activity Sheet

PROCEDURE:
1. Copy and laminate for durability one copy of Teacher Time Saver.
2. Place a container of fish-shaped crackers in the center.

Ask parents to send in a supply of these fish-shaped crackers.

3. Supply glue and pencil.

TEACHER DIRECTIONS TO STUDENTS:
1. Read each problem on the laminated sheet.
2. Write the number story on the tail of each fish.
3. Write the answer and glue the crackers onto the fish to show your answer. The first one shows you what to do.
4. When you are finished, count to see what the greatest answer was. You may eat that many fish crackers!

CONTENT HINT: *Science*

Use with a unit about fish, pond life, or oceans.

Name _____ **Date** _____

Gone Fishing

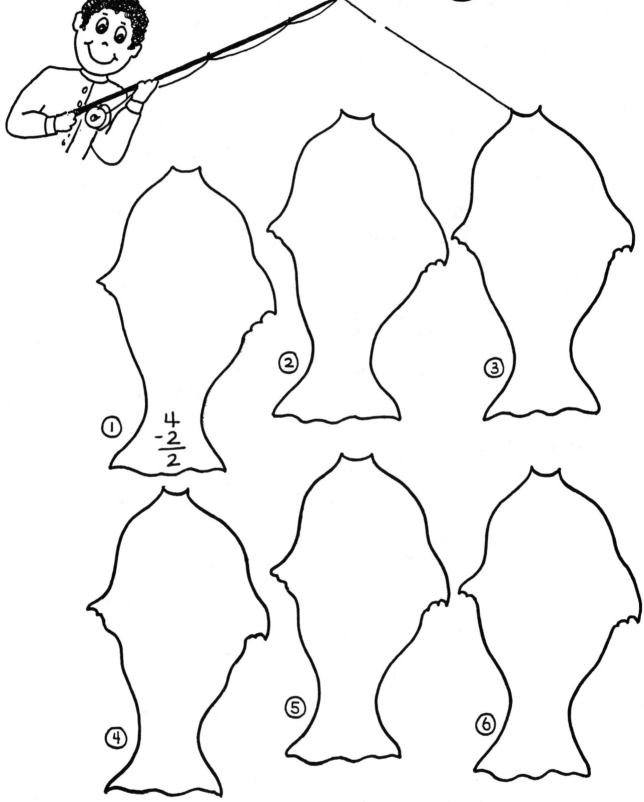

$$\begin{array}{r} 4 \\ -2 \\ \hline 2 \end{array}$$

Student Activity Sheet

Gone Fishing

Jill went fishing. She caught four fish. Two swam away. How many were left?	Bob snagged nine fish, but three got away. How many did he have then?
Tom hooked five fish. No fish got away from him. How many did he take home?	Tina caught eight fish in her net. Two fish jumped back into the pond. How many fish did she keep?
Kevin fished from his boat. He got ten fish on the line. But eight fish fell off. How many fish did he pull into the boat?	Carlos hooked nine fish in the pond. Three fell into the water. How many did Carlos have then?

Teacher Time Saver

ZAP THOSE BUGS

OBJECTIVE: Students will subtract and show the answer by using tongue depressors and macaroni.

MATERIALS: Tongue depressors

Macaroni (or brown beans)

Crayons

Scissors

Glue

Copies of Frog Teacher Time Saver

PROCEDURE:
1. Copy a frog for each student.
2. Cut tongue depressors in half.
3. Put macaroni or beans in a can or container.
4. Supply scissors, crayons, and glue.

TEACHER DIRECTIONS TO STUDENTS:
1. Color and cut out the hungry frog.
2. Write a subtraction fact on one side of a tongue depressor.
3. Using the macaroni or beans for bugs, show the answer to the problem by gluing them to the other side of the tongue depressor. You may use two tongue depressors.
4. Feed your frog!

CONTENT HINT: *Science*

Use with a unit about amphibians or insects.

Zap Those Bugs

Teacher Time Saver

THE COOKIE CHEF

OBJECTIVE: Students will be able to make a line graph and use it in doing subtraction problems.

MATERIALS: Student Activity Sheet

Ruler

Manipulative objects (optional)

PROCEDURE:
1. Duplicate student activity sheet for each student.
2. Provide a ruler and a pencil.

*This activity should be done independently only after line graphs have been introduced to students and they have had practice as a group making and interpreting them.

TEACHER DIRECTIONS TO STUDENTS:
1. Make dots on lines to show how many cookies were baked each day.
2. Connect the dots to make a line graph.
3. Read the story problems and write the number problem and answer.

The Cookie Chef

Put dots on the lines to show how many cookies were baked. Connect the dots.

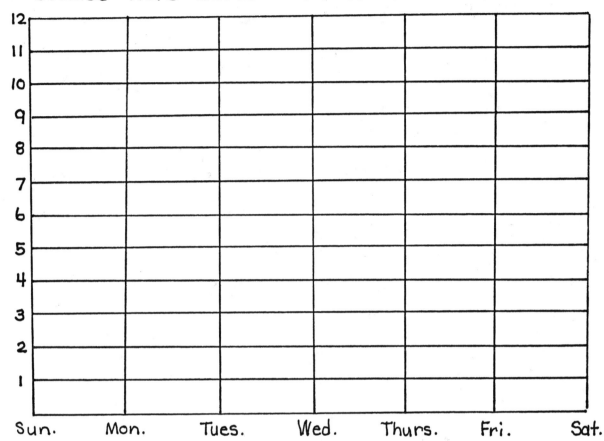

	Sun.	Mon.	Tues.	Wed.	Thurs.	Fri.	Sat.
12							
11							
10							
9							
8							
7							
6							
5							
4							
3							
2							
1							

Chef Alan baked:

6 dozen on Sunday
2 dozen on Monday
10 dozen on Tuesday
8 dozen on Wednesday
3 dozen on Thursday
11 dozen on Friday
1 dozen on Saturday

Write the problem and answers:

1. How many more did he bake on Tuesday than on Monday?
2. How many more did he bake on Friday than on Thursday?
3. How many more did he bake on Wednesday than on Saturday?

Student Activity Sheet

Place Value

BEAN-O

OBJECTIVE: Students will demonstrate understanding of beginning place value by making sets of tens with remaining ones using tongue depressors and beans.

MATERIALS: Tongue depressors

Small beans such as pinto

Glue

Student Activity Sheet

PROCEDURE:
1. Put beans into a butter tub.
2. Tongue depressors fit easily in an empty coffee can or small oatmeal box.
3. Make a stack of cards with numbers printed on them such as:

TEACHER DIRECTIONS TO STUDENTS:
1. Choose a card from the stack.
2. Take one tongue depressor for each ten in the number.
3. Glue ten beans on each stick.
4. Lay the beans beside the sticks to show the ones.
5. On the Student Activity Sheet trace each stick to represent the tens and draw ten beans on each. Draw the beans to represent the ones beside the tens. Don't forget to record the number that was on your card.
6. Leave your sets on the counter (or appropriate place) to dry.

 Save the sets for use in counting tens, combining to make hundreds, or for children to work in pairs for cooperative learning activity.

CONTENT HINT: Use with the story of *Jack and the Beanstalk.* Tongue depressors can be sprayed with green paint ahead of time to create the "pods" for the beans.

Bean-O

Name _____

Date _____

Student Activity Sheet

STRINGING TENS

OBJECTIVE: Students will make sets of ten.

MATERIALS: Oat cereal such as Cheerios™
Pipe cleaners
Student Activity Sheet

PROCEDURE:
1. Pour cereal into a large butter tub or similar container.
2. Cut pipe cleaners in half, or if they are extra long cut into thirds. Put in a container.
3. Make a stack of cards with tens printed on them such as:

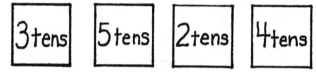

Place face down in a pile.
4. Copy one Student Activity Sheet for each child.

TEACHER DIRECTIONS TO STUDENTS:
1. Choose three cards from the stack of ten cards.
2. Read a card and take one pipe cleaner for each ten.
3. Put ten pieces of cereal on each pipe cleaner and curl the end of the pipe cleaner to keep the cereal from slipping off.
4. Record what you found in your set on the Student Activity Sheet.
5. One example has been done for you.
6. You may keep the sets you made.

Stringing Tens

Name _____
Date _____

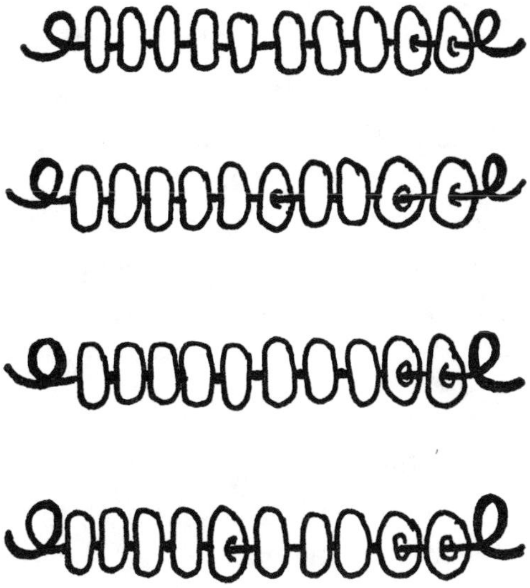

4 tens = ☐

___ tens = ☐

___ tens = ☐

___ tens = ☐

Student Activity Sheet

BUTTONS BUTTONS

OBJECTIVE: Students will make sets of tens and ones using buttons.

MATERIALS: 99 buttons

Nine Ziploc™ sandwich bags

Stack of number cards above ten

Student Activity Sheet

PROCEDURE:
1. Put buttons in a butter tub.
2. Make number cards for a pile from which the students can draw. Ex:

 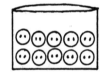 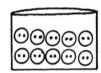

| 43 | 67 | 93 | 86 | 52 | 38 | 29 |

3. Put out nine Ziploc™ bags or sandwich bags with twist ties to hold them closed.
4. Reproduce one Student Activity Sheet for each child.

TEACHER DIRECTIONS TO STUDENTS:
1. Choose a card from the number card stack.
2. Make the set by putting ten buttons in a bag to represent each ten and lay single buttons beside the bags to represent the ones.
3. Example:

4. Practice several times, then do the Student Activity Sheet.

Buttons Buttons

Draw bags of buttons to show tens and ones.

| 46 | | 25 |

| 53 | | 17 |

TRAIN RIDE

OBJECTIVE: Students will demonstrate knowledge of place value with a milk carton train and straws.

MATERIALS: Six to eight milk cartons or similar size boxes

Straws and rubberbands (used in Bundle Up Activities)

Student Activity Sheet

PROCEDURE:
1. With help from children, aid or parent volunteer make a train from the milk cartons or boxes—be as creative as you like!
2. Put a number on each train car. Example:

3. Cut straws in half (you may have already done so if this activity follows "Bundle Up".)

TEACHER DIRECTIONS TO STUDENTS:
1. Using straws make bundles of tens and ones and put in each car of the train.
2. Show your work on the Student Activity Sheet by using the symbols:

$$\phi \;=\; 1 \text{ bundle of } 10$$

$$1 \;=\; 1 \text{ one}$$

Example:

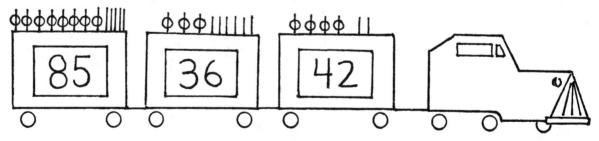

CONTENT HINT: This is a good activity to use with a transportation unit in Social Studies. Students can create their own trains for this activity using a wide variety of materials.

Name _____ **Date** _____

Train Ride

Draw sets for the numbers on the train. Use φ for each ten and 1 for each one.

Student Activity Sheet

BUNDLE UP

OBJECTIVE: Students will be able to make sets of tens and hundreds by using straws and rubber bands.

MATERIALS: One box of paper drinking straws

Basket or plastic tub

Rubber bands

Student Activity Sheet

PROCEDURE:
1. Cut straws in half and place in a large basket or plastic tub.
2. Rubber bands fit neatly in a butter tub.
3. Duplicate Student Activity Sheet for each student.
4. Duplicate one copy of Teacher Time Saver and cut apart. Put into a ziplock bag or butter tub.

TEACHER DIRECTIONS TO STUDENTS:
1. Choose four number cards from the bag or tub.
2. Using the straws, put rubber bands around sets of tens and hundreds where appropriate.
3. Record your sets on the Student Activity Sheet. Use the following symbols:

ϕ = 10 (1 stick in a circle)

⦀⦀⦀ = 100 (10 sticks in a circle)

| = (1 stick for each one)

4. Here is an example for you to follow. Prepare ahead of time six bundles of ten and three ones along with a card that shows:

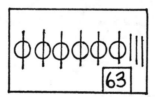

Also demonstrate how you would put a large rubber band around ten sets of ten to make 100. Show an example and a prepared card such as:

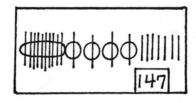

82

Name _____ Date _____

Bundle Up

Bundle Up

143	96
84	135
162	247
189	39
92	178
238	264
68	127
73	154

HAT TRICKS

OBJECTIVE: Students will demonstrate knowledge of place value by creating a funny hat using construction paper, colored cereal, and other art supplies.

MATERIALS: Various colors of 12″ circles cut in half

Colored cereal such as Trix™

Ruler

Scraps of yarn

Sequins

Glitter

Scraps of colored tissue

Scraps of construction paper

Foil

Ribbons

PROCEDURE:
1. Cut 12″ circles of various colors of construction paper. Then cut them in half.
2. Prepare slips of paper with numerals of your choice, ex:

$$\boxed{46} \quad \boxed{31} \quad \boxed{16} \quad \boxed{27}$$

fold in half, and put in butter tub.
3. Pour cereal into container such as a basket.
4. Provide art box containing interesting materials—paper, ribbons, sequins, etc.
5. Provide a ruler, glue, and scissors.

1. Choose a half circle of construction paper for the basic part of your hat.

2. Draw a numbered slip of paper from the butter tub.

3. Decide how many tens there are in the number.

4. Using the ruler line off a section for each ten on your hat.
   Example:

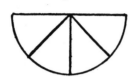

   (You need 4 sections)

5. Now fold your hat around and glue it in the shape of a cone.

6. Glue ten pieces of cereal in each section to represent a set of 10. The extra "ones" are glued near the point.

7. To complete your hat, use the art box to create your own idea of a great hat.

8. Show your hat to your teacher to explain your placement of tens and ones. Your teacher will staple two pieces of yarn to your hat if you wish to wear it.

Make a model of a hat to share with your class. If you connect it with a holiday you may want to use colors that reflect the holiday such as orange and black for Halloween or green and orange for St. Patrick's Day.

Example:

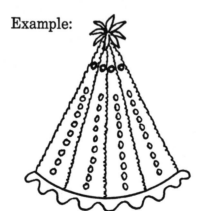

Black with gold glitter and orange crepe paper at bottom, foil spikes at top, and cereal balls to represent sets of tens.

GUMDROP FUN

OBJECTIVE: Students will work in groups of four to complete a line graph with place value.

MATERIALS: 5 lbs. of gumdrops for 24 children

Plastic bags

Crayons

Pencils

Wax paper

PROCEDURE:
1. Divide the gumdrops into six bags (if there are 24 children).
2. Arrange students in teams of four.
3. Give each team a bag of gumdrops, a sheet of wax paper, and a graph sheet.

TEACHER DIRECTIONS TO STUDENTS:
1. Your team is to group the gumdrops according to color.
2. Then group them in sets of tens and ones.
3. Record your amount of each color of gumdrops by using the same color of crayon. (Demonstrate.)

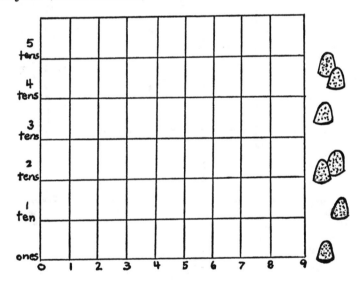

4. Work through the graph questions at the bottom of the page. When you have completed all parts, raise your hand and share with the teacher.

When you are finished make a large graph for the class where you combine all answers. You may need to use hundreds on your class graph.

CONTENT HINT: Use with a holiday unit around Christmas time when color gumdrops are available.

Name _____ Date _____

Gumdrop Fun

Draw a line using the same color as the gumdrops to show how many.

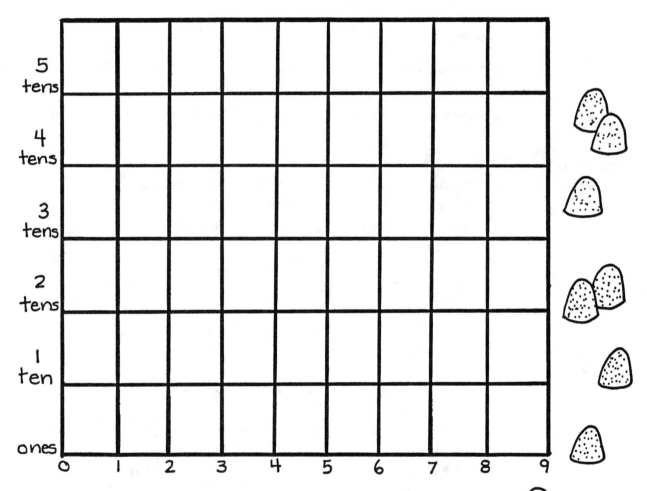

How many red gumdrops? _____
Which color had the most? _____
Which color had the least? _____
What is the difference between yellow and red? _____
What is the difference between purple and white? _____
Divide the gumdrops so that each person in your
  group has the same amount. How many does each
  person have? _____
Beside your name at the top use a crayon to
  make a dot to show your favorite.

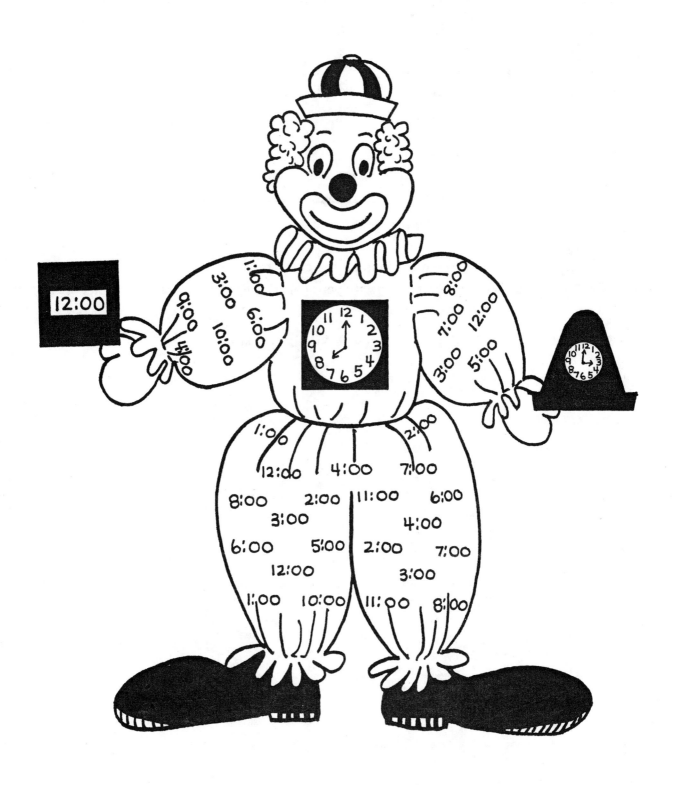

Telling Time

TICK-TOCK-CLOCK

OBJECTIVE: Students will be able to make a simple clock face and put the numerals in the appropriate places.

MATERIALS: Paper plates

Markers or crayons

Brass fasteners

Construction paper

Scissors

PROCEDURE:
1. Copy Teacher Time Saver and put in the center or enlarge onto posterboard.
2. Make a pattern to be traced for the clock hands.

TEACHER DIRECTIONS TO STUDENTS:
1. Follow the directions on the chart to make your clock.
2. Write the numerals with your pencil and then trace with the color of marker you like.

CONTENT HINT: Use with the nursery rhyme "Hickory, Dickory, Dock."

①
- On your paper plate write the numerals 12 and 6. Make sure they are in a straight line from top to bottom.

- Trace the numerals with your favorite color.

②
- On your clock write the numerals 9 and 3. Make sure they are in a straight line from left to right.

- Trace the numerals in your favorite color.

③
- Fill in the missing numerals. Make sure they are spaced evenly.

- Trace the numerals with your favorite color.

④
- Trace the pattern for the hands of the clock. Choose a color you like.
- Cut out the hands and put the brass fasteners through them.
- Push the fastener through the center of the clock.

MY TIME

OBJECTIVE: Students will demonstrate an understanding of time by drawing pictures of things they do at given times of day.

MATERIALS: Pencils
Colored pencils
Teacher Time Saver
Student Activity Sheet

PROCEDURE:
1. Duplicate Teacher Time Saver and cut apart. Fold pieces and put in a butter tub or basket.
2. Copy the Student Activity Sheet for each student.
3. Supply colored pencils.

TEACHER DIRECTIONS TO STUDENTS:
1. Choose four slips of paper from the tub.
2. Write a time in each box of your Student Activity Sheet. Don't forget to put A.M. or P.M.
3. Fold the slips again and return to the tub.
4. Draw a picture to show what you do on a school day for each time you wrote.
5. Use the colored pencils to complete your pictures.

CONTENT HINT: Use with a Health Unit about healthy habits (eating proper meals, getting enough rest and exercise, and good grooming).

My Time

Name _____ Date _____

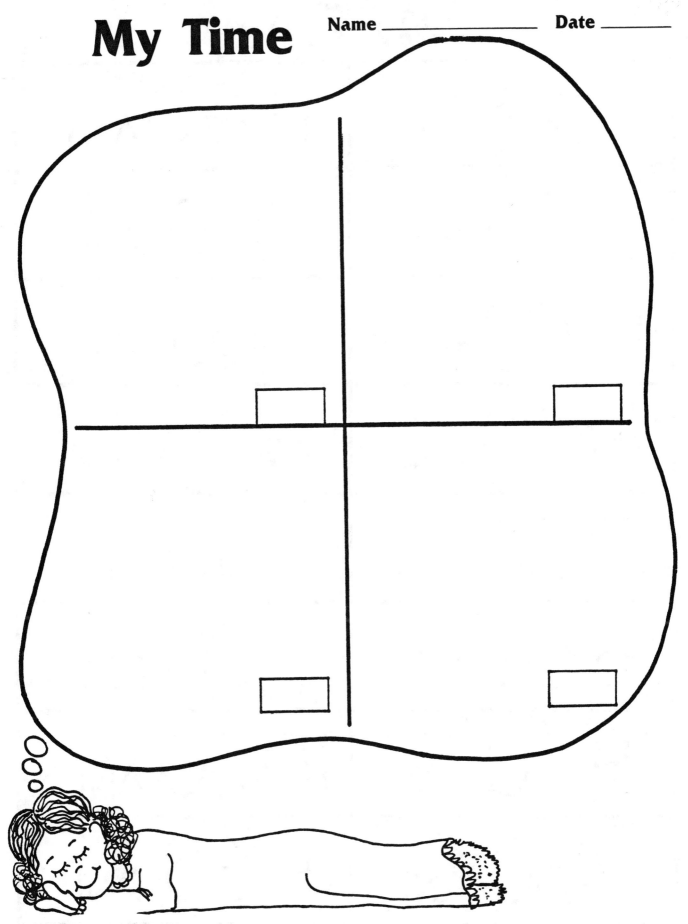

Student Activity Sheet

My Time

1:00 PM	11:00 AM
3:30 PM	8:00 AM
12:00 NOON	9:00 PM
4:00 AM	6:00 AM
7:00 AM	5:30 PM
6:00 PM	2:00 PM
9:00 AM	10:00 AM
7:30 AM	4:30 PM

Teacher Time Saver

CLOCK PUZZLES

OBJECTIVE: Students will draw the hands on a clock when given a specific time for hours, half hour, and quarter hour.

MATERIALS: Pencil

Glue

Scissors

9″ × 12″ construction paper

Ziplock bag

Student Activity Sheet

PROCEDURE:
1. Duplicate the Teacher Time Saver, paste onto colored construction paper, and cut apart to make puzzles. Laminate for durability.
2. Copy the Student Activity Sheet for each student.

TEACHER DIRECTIONS TO STUDENTS:
1. First match up the times on the clock puzzles and have a friend check it for you.
2. On your Student Activity Sheet read the digital times and draw the hands of the clock to show the same time.
3. Show it to your teacher.
4. Glue the entire sheet onto a piece of construction paper and let dry.
5. Cut puzzle pieces apart and keep in a Baggie.

Clock Puzzles

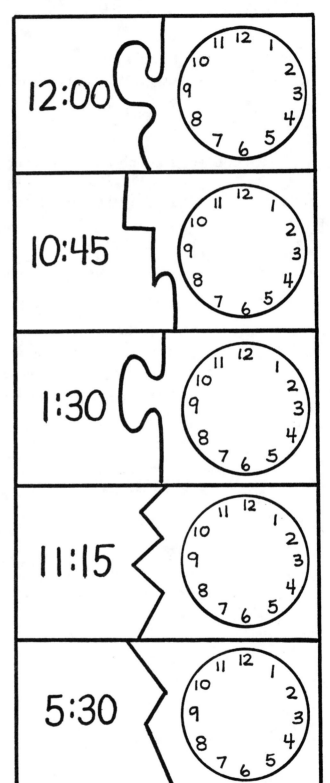

Clock Puzzles

7:30	half past seven
10:00	ten o'clock
8:15	fifteen minutes past eight o'clock
1:00	one o'clock
3:30	half past three

2:00	two o'clock
9:45	forty-five minutes after nine
12:00	noon or midnight
5:30	half past five
11:45	fifteen minutes past eleven

CUDDLY CLOCKS

OBJECTIVE: Students will write time to the five minutes on clock faces.

MATERIALS: Pencil
Teacher Time Saver
Student Activity Sheet

PROCEDURE:
1. Duplicate the Teacher Time Saver and cut apart.
2. Copy a Student Activity Sheet for each child.

TEACHER DIRECTIONS TO STUDENTS:
1. Choose six cards from the stack.
2. Read each time and write the digital time in the digital box.
3. Put the hands on the clock to show the digital time.

 The Teacher may wish to change some of the times to adapt to the level of the class.

A clock with moveable hands is helpful in the center.

CONTENT HINT: Use with a unit about pets, farm animals, or animals.

Name _____ Date _____

Cuddly Clocks

Cuddly Clocks

Five minutes past three	Seven thirty
Eleven o'clock	Half past two
Six forty-five	Twelve twenty
One fifty	Four fifteen
Ten minutes past six	Noon
Eight thirty	Ten thirty
Nine o'clock	Half past three

TIME'S UP!

OBJECTIVE: Students will complete given tasks in a given amount of time.

MATERIALS: Egg timer or a timer you can set the time
24″ lengths of yarn
Pencil
Hole punch
Scissors
Student Activity Sheet

PROCEDURE:
1. Provide an egg timer and instruct the students in how to set it.
2. Cut a 24″ length of yarn for each student.
3. Duplicate the Student Activity Sheet for each student.
4. Adjust the time to suit your class.

TEACHER DIRECTIONS TO STUDENTS:
1. Make sure you know how to use the timer. Set it for three minutes before doing circles 1, 2, and 3.
2. Read the directions for 4 carefully and follow directions to make your necklace.

Time's Up

①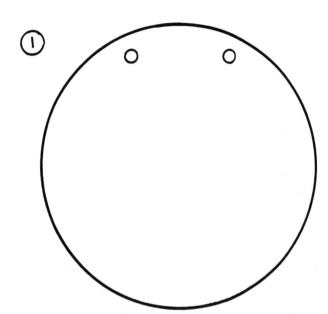

Write as many words as you can that begin with "a."

②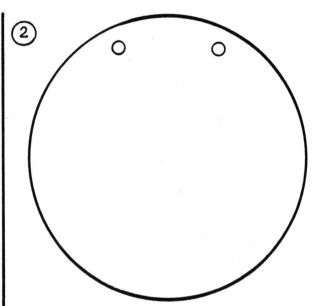

Draw a crazy monster.

③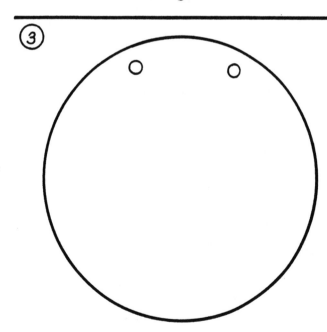

Put the numerals on the clock. Make the hands show two hours past noon.

④

In
3 Minutes
Time

Now take your time and cut out the four circles. Use the hole punch to make holes. Put yarn through to make a necklace.

© 1992 by The Center for Applied Research in Education, Inc.

SWEET DREAMS

OBJECTIVE: Students will record and interpret time using a bar graph.

MATERIALS: The time each student in the class goes to bed.
Pencil
Crayons
Student Activity Sheet

PROCEDURE:
1. Give each child a slip of paper and ask that the name and bedtime be written on it.
2. Put the slips of paper in a box, butter tub, baggie, or basket for use in the center.
3. Copy the Student Activity Sheet for each child.

TEACHER DIRECTIONS TO STUDENTS:
1. Take out all the slips of paper with the bedtimes on them.
2. Fill in a graph space for each slip above the appropriate time. You may use the color of crayon you choose.
3. Return each slip to the basket as you record the time.
4. Answer all the questions below the graph.

CONTENT HINT: Use with a Health Unit on the body—getting enough rest and sleep or healthy habits.

Sweet Dreams

What time do most students go to bed? _____
What time do fewest students go to bed? _____
What time do you go to bed? _____
How many students go to bed at 10:00? _____
How many students go to bed later than 10:00? _____
Do more students go to bed at 8:00 or 9:30? _____
What time do you go to bed on the weekends? _____

Student Activity Sheet

Money

PENNIES PLEASE

OBJECTIVE: Students will trace a nickel and pennies to show money less than 10¢.

MATERIALS: One nickel
Three pennies
Large paper pennies and a nickel
Student Activity Sheet
Clear self-stick vinyl

PROCEDURE:
1. Enlarge Student Activity Sheet and laminate for center.
2. Purchase or make large paper pennies and a nickel.
3. Copy Student Activity Sheet.

TEACHER DIRECTIONS TO STUDENTS:
1. Practice putting the coins on the chart Pennies Please.
2. When you feel that you have put the correct amount of money on, use the real coins to trace the amount on the Student Activity Sheet.

CONTENT HINT: Use this activity when you begin work on money. Coordinate it with any Social Studies, Science, Health, or Seasonal Unit.

Name _____ Date _____

Pennies Please

SOMETHING FISHY

OBJECTIVE: Students will choose a money problem whose value is 50¢ or less and interpret the problem using nickels.

MATERIALS: Ten nickels (real or play money)
Pencil and crayons
Fish bowl
Teacher Time Saver
Student Activity Sheet

PROCEDURE:
1. Copy, color, and cut out fish from Teacher Time Saver.
2. Cut out the money cards, fold in half, and put in the fish bowl.
3. Duplicate Student Activity Sheet for each student.
4. Put real or play nickels in a butter tub

TEACHER DIRECTIONS TO STUDENTS:
1. Choose a money card from the fish bowl. Write the amount on your Student Activity Sheet and put the card back in the bowl.
2. Use the nickels to count the money on your card. Put a fish with each nickel you use to see how many fish you can buy for your money.

Example: 15¢   You could buy 3 fish.

3. Draw the fish you can buy in the bowl on the Student Activity Sheet.
4. Color and decorate any way you wish!

CONTENT HINT: Coordinate with a unit about fish, the ocean, or environment. This is also good to use with books such as *Swimmy* by Leo Lionni.

Something Fishy

How many fish can you buy for ___ if each one costs 5¢?

I can buy ___ fish.

Something Fishy

5¢	10¢	15¢
20¢	25¢	30¢
35¢	40¢	45¢
50¢		

ICE CREAM SHOP

OBJECTIVE: Students will use money stamps to show how much money the items in the shop costs.

MATERIALS: Rubber money stamps

Ink pad

[Alternative—coins to trace and draw]

Student Activity Sheet

Scrap paper

Tub of play money

PROCEDURE:
1. Supply money stamps and ink pads, and scrap paper to practice on.
2. If needed, you may put a dime, quarter, nickel and penny in a cup for students to trace and draw their answers.
3. Put a tub of play coins in the center.
4. Copy Student Activity Sheet for each student.

TEACHER DIRECTIONS TO STUDENTS:
1. Practice making coins on the scrap paper before you print your answers
2. Lay out the play money to make sure you have the correct amount of coins.
3. Choose the correct stamps to stamp your paper.

CONTENT HINT: Use with a unit about food or when talking about Summer Fun Activities.

Ice Cream Shop

 97¢

 62¢

 81¢

 53¢

Student Activity Sheet

BASKET OF EGGS

OBJECTIVE: Students will count money to 99¢, compute cost of items, and determine change.

MATERIALS: Plastic eggs from hosiery
Basket
Wrapped hard candy
Play or real money
Student Activity Sheet

PROCEDURE:
1. Use at least four plastic eggs—eight works very well.
2. Tape a number to the outside of each egg.
3. Put several pieces of wrapped hard candy and some real or play money into each egg. (Money should be between 50¢ and 99¢.)
4. Copy the Student Activity Sheet for each student.

TEACHER DIRECTIONS TO STUDENTS:
1. Choose an egg from the basket.
2. Write the number of the egg on the egg in the first box of the Activity Sheet.
3. Open the egg and count the money. Write it in the space in the first box.
4. Read each questions and fill in the answers.
5. Make sure you return the candy and money to the egg and close it tight before replacing it in the basket.

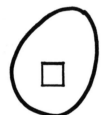

Name _____ Date _____

Basket of Eggs

Choose four eggs. Count the money and answer the questions.

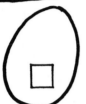 You have
_____ ¢.

Each piece of candy costs
2¢. How much does
the candy cost? _____ ¢

How much change will
you get back? _____ ¢

 You have
_____ ¢.

Each piece of candy costs
1¢. How much does
the candy cost? _____ ¢

How much change will
you get back? _____ ¢

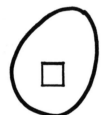 You have
_____ ¢

Each piece of candy costs
3¢. How much does
the candy cost? _____ ¢

How much change will
you get back? _____ ¢

 You have
_____ ¢

Each piece of candy costs
5¢. How much does
the candy cost? _____ ¢

How much change will
you get back? _____ ¢

Student Activity Sheet

SHOPPING BASKET

OBJECTIVE: Students will compute the cost of items and make change.

MATERIALS: Basket (preferably with handles)

Items such as:
  Small stuffed animals
  Pencil
  Book
  Small toys
  Jewelry
  Box of crayons
  Ruler
Eight envelopes
Student Activity Sheet

PROCEDURE:
1. Put a price tag on each item.
2. Put a number on each item (1–15 if you have 15 items). Put items in the basket.
3. In each envelope put the numbers of three items and number the outside of the envelope.
4. On one copy of the Student Activity Sheet write the amount of money the student has to spend.
5. Make a copy of the Student Activity Sheet for each student.

TEACHER DIRECTIONS TO STUDENTS:
1. Choose one of the 8 envelopes.
2. Read the numbers in the envelope and remove those items from the shopping basket.
3. On your Student Activity Sheet write the envelope number on the picture of the envelope.
4. Draw a picture of each item and write how much it cost.
5. Total the items to see how much you spent.
6. Subtract the total from the amount you had to begin with to see how much change you have.

 Teachers can price items and money to begin with to suit the level of the students.

Shopping Basket

You have ____. You chose ⬜.
You buy:

a _____ for _____

a _____ for _____

a _____ for _____

You spent _____.

You get _____ change.

© 1992 by The Center for Applied Research in Education, Inc.

PIGGY BANKS

OBJECTIVE: Kindergarten students will become aware of saving money by making a piggy bank.

MATERIALS: Butter tubs
Pipe cleaners
Teacher Time Saver
Pink construction paper
Glue

PROCEDURE:
1. Copy the Teacher Time Saver onto pink construction paper and cut apart.
2. Cut pipe cleaners in half.
3. Poke a hole in one side of butter tubs.
4. Cut a slit in lid of butter tub.

TEACHER DIRECTIONS TO STUDENTS:
1. Cut out a pig face and decorate it with your crayons. Glue it onto the butter tub.
2. Twist the pipe cleaner around a pencil or crayon and insert in the hole at the side of the butter tub.
3. Take it home to save your money!

Example:

Piggy Banks

CHANGE PURSES

OBJECTIVE: Students will be able to count and record money to 99¢.

MATERIALS: Four change purses
Play or real coins
Student Activity Sheet

PROCEDURE:
1. Purchase or ask that four small, zippered change purses be donated to the class.
2. Decide how much real or play money you want in each purse and put it in. Tag each purse with numbers 1–4.
3. Duplicate Student Activity Sheet.

TEACHER DIRECTIONS TO STUDENTS:
1. Choose purse number one. Look at the coins and record the information on your Student Activity Sheet.
2. Count the coins asked for in each square and record the total amount of money for those two kinds of coins.

CONTENT HINT: Coordinate this activity with a unit about pets. Have students bring stuffed animals and labels for pet supplies or real items such as a leash, bird food, or flea collar.

Also use when you study Community Helpers. Set up a grocery store with empty cans and boxes for the shelves. A cash register or box for money allows students to work in pairs buying and selling at the store.

Change Purses

1

¢

How many pennies? ___
How many nickels? ___
How many dimes? ___
How many quarters? ___
___ nickels + ___ dimes
is _____ ¢

2

¢

How many pennies? ___
How many nickels? ___
How many dimes? ___
How many quarters? ___
___ pennies + ___ nickels
is _____ ¢

3

¢

How many pennies? ___
How many nickels? ___
How many dimes? ___
How many quarters? ___
___ dimes + ___ pennies
is _____ ¢

4

¢

How many pennies? ___
How many nickels? ___
How many dimes? ___
How many quarters? ___
___ quarters + ___ pennies
is _____ ¢

© 1992 by The Center for Applied Research in Education, Inc.

ALLOWANCE DAY

OBJECTIVE: Students will become aware of how much money their fellow students get for allowance, how much of it they can spend and how much they save.

MATERIALS: 3″ × 3″ slips of paper

Basket, large butter tub or box

Student Activity Sheet

Crayons and pencil

PROCEDURE:
1. Pass out 3″ × 3″ paper to each student.
2. Have them write:

                    First name _____

                    Allowance _____

                    Save _____

                    Spend_____

3. They then fold it and put it in the container.
4. Copy a Student Activity Sheet for each student.

 If putting names on the paper is a problem for your class or you feel it could be embarrassing, then ask them to make up a name of someone who is not in the room. You may even wish to omit name and put a number on each card yourself.

TEACHER DIRECTIONS TO STUDENTS:
1. Choose five cards from the basket.
2. Record the information on the Student Activity Sheet.
3. Color the information onto the graph and answer the questions.

Allowance Day

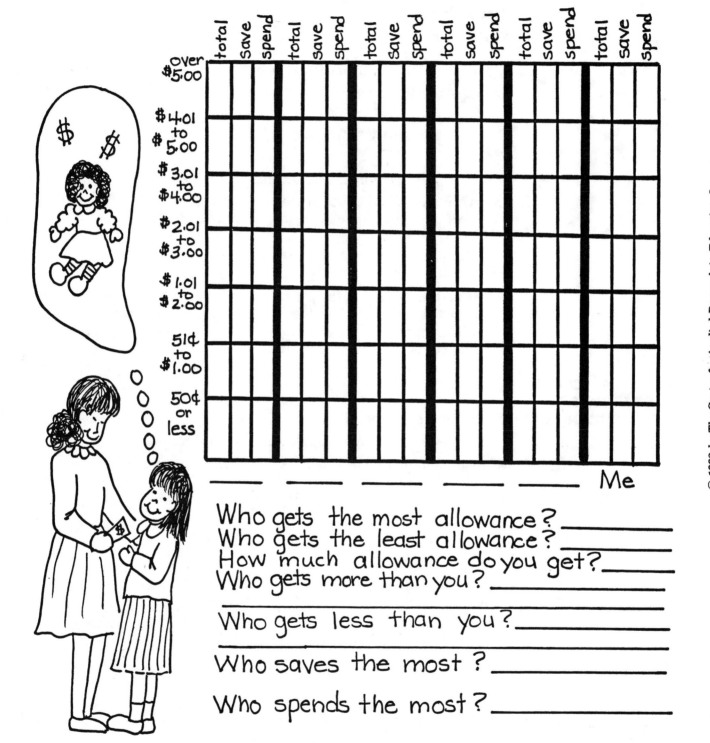

	total	save	spend	total	save	spend	total	save	spend	total	save	spend	total	save	spend	total	save	spend
over $5.00																		
$4.01 to $5.00																		
$3.01 to $4.00																		
$2.01 to $3.00																		
$1.01 to $2.00																		
51¢ to $1.00																		
50¢ or less																		

___ ___ ___ ___ ___ ___ Me

Who gets the most allowance? _____

Who gets the least allowance? _____

How much allowance do you get? _____

Who gets more than you? _____

Who gets less than you? _____

Who saves the most? _____

Who spends the most? _____

Student Activity Sheet

Measurement

CHEERIO!

OBJECTIVE: Students will measure in centimeters using oat cereal.

MATERIALS: Oat cereal
Pencil
Student Activity Sheet

PROCEDURE:
1. Put oat cereal in a large plastic butter tub. Put some in small plastic Baggies.
2. Duplicate Student Activity Sheet for each student.

TEACHER DIRECTIONS TO STUDENTS:
1. Put the oat cereal close together on the worms for the birds.
2. Write how many pieces it took to fill the worm.
3. Read how long it was.
4. When you finish you may eat your cereal.
5. Take a Baggie of cereal and your paper home to show your family how to do it.

Good for kindergarten and first grade. It can be used as a whole class activity when discussing centimeters.

CONTENT HINT: Use with a unit about birds or spring.

Name _____   Date _____

Cheerio!

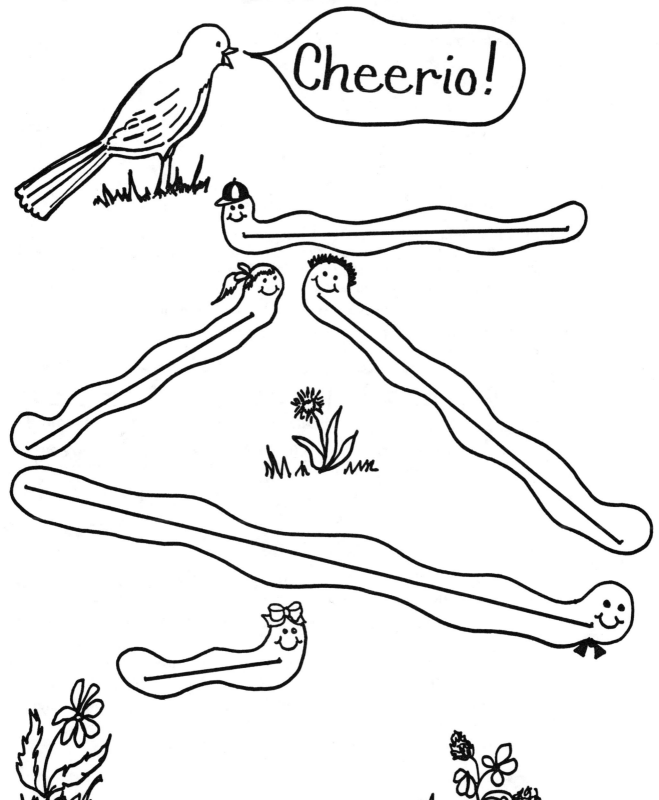

Student Activity Sheet

HOT, WARM OR COLD

OBJECTIVE: Students will use a cooking thermometer to measure the temperature of various liquids.

MATERIALS: Cooking thermometer
Ice bucket and ice
Plastic cups/styrofoam cups
Water
Thermos with warm water
Hot chocolate mix
Powdered drink mix
Teaspoon
Student Activity Sheet

PROCEDURE:
1. In the center put a plastic bottle of room temperature water, a thermos of very warm water, an ice bucket with ice cubes, a butter tub with hot chocolate mix, a butter tub with powdered drink mix such as lemonade or Kool-Aid™, a teaspoon, cups and thermometer.
2. Duplicate Student Activity Sheet for each student.
3. Put the following labels on three cups.

TEACHER DIRECTIONS TO STUDENTS:
1. Pour some water from the plastic bottle into cup number 1. Measure and record the temperature.
2. Put water into cup number 2. Add an ice cube. Measure and record the temperature.
3. Pour some water from the thermos into cup number 3. Measure and record the temperature.
4. Decide which drink you would prefer, and choose the appropriate water to make that drink.
5. Answer the questions on the Student Activity Sheet.

126

Hot, Warm, or Cold

Pour water into cup 1.
Measure the temperature. 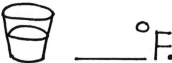 _____ °F.

Pour water from cup 1 into cup 2. Add ice cubes. Now what is the temperature?  _____ °F.

Pour water from the thermos into cup 3. Measure the temperature.  _____ °F.

You may make hot chocolate or lemonade. Choose. Put 3 teaspoons of the mix you chose into a new cup. Which water will you need? _____ °F. Do you need to add ice? _____

Write the temperatures you recorded above. Then write two drinks that are good at that temperature.

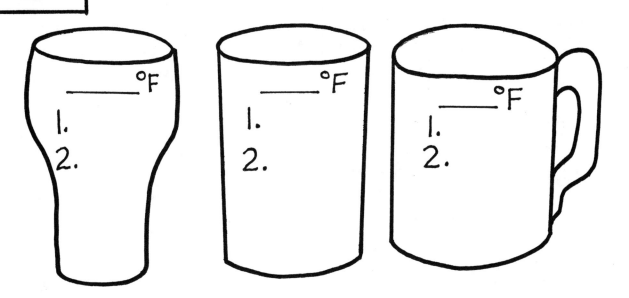

Student Activity Sheet

ELF'S RICE

OBJECTIVE: Students will measure volume using tablespoons, cups, pints, quarts, gallons, and green rice.

MATERIALS: Large plastic tub
Two gallons rice
Green food coloring
Rubbing alcohol
Tablespoon
Plastic 1-cup measuring cup
Pint container or measuring cup
Quart container
Gallon measuring container
Student Activity Sheet

Ask parents to contribute bags of long cooking rice.

PROCEDURE:
1. Put about 4 or 5 tablespoons of rubbing alcohol and a few drops of green food coloring into a plastic container with a lid (Ziploc.™ bags work also), add rice and shake. Pour into large plastic tub. Repeat until you have colored all rice.
2. Provide measuring containers and label them.
3. Reproduce Student Activity Sheet for each student.

TEACHER DIRECTIONS TO STUDENTS:
1 Make sure you do all your measuring over the large tub. Rice on the floor can be slippery.
2. Follow the dirctions on the Student Activity Sheet and record your answers.

CONTENT HINT: Use this activity in March, near St. Patrick's Day, or when you study elves, gnomes, or trolls in a literature setting.

Elf's Rice

Name _____

Date _____

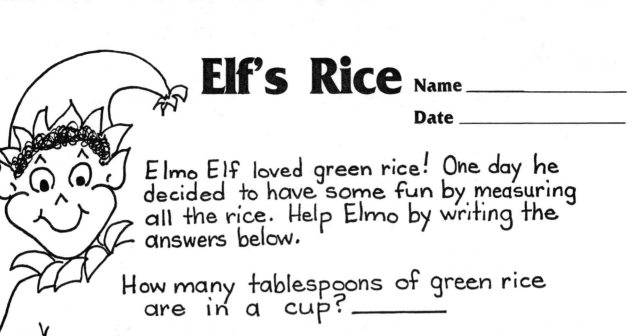

Elmo Elf loved green rice! One day he decided to have some fun by measuring all the rice. Help Elmo by writing the answers below.

How many tablespoons of green rice are in a cup? _____

How many cups of green rice can you put in a pint? _____

How many pints of green rice are in a quart? _____

How many quarts of green rice are in a gallon? _____

How many cups of green rice are in a quart? _____

How many pints of green rice are in a gallon? _____

How many cups of green rice are in a gallon? _____

Which is more: a cup or a quart? _____

Which is less: a quart or a gallon? _____

Student Activity Sheet

HIGH FLIER

OBJECTIVE: Students will create a kite by following directions in measuring with inches.

MATERIALS: Yarn

Construction paper

Wallpaper book

Ruler with inches

Scissors

Glue

A penny

Teacher Time Saver (two pages)

PROCEDURE:
1. Reproduce the Teacher Time Saver pages and put on a chart in the center.
2. Make available various colors of 9″ × 12″ construction paper, a wallpaper book, and yarn that has not been cut into lengths.
3. Students should be very familiar with the use of a ruler in order to be successful.

TEACHER DIRECTIONS TO STUDENTS:
1. Look at the directions carefully on the chart.
2. You may use the colors of paper and yarn you wish to make your kite.
3. Use the wallpaper book to make the bows for the tail of the kite.

For advanced children you may add the directions: Make a kite by doubling the measurements on the chart.

For this you would need to have larger paper available.

CONTENT HINT: Use with a unit about March, Spring, or Wind. Many books are available in the library to extend the activity into the literature you use.

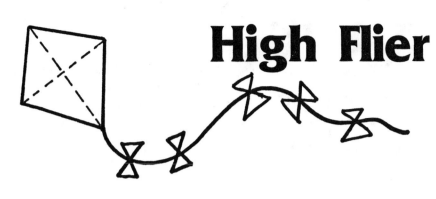

High Flier

1. On each 9" end of the paper make a dot at the 4½" mark. Draw a dotted line to connect the two dots. Label them A and B.

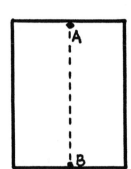

2. On each 12" side of the paper make a dot at the 5" mark. Draw a dotted line to connect the two dots. Label them C and D.

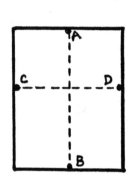

3. Draw a solid line to connect dots A and C. Draw a solid line to connect dots A and D. Draw a solid line to connect B and C. Draw a solid line to connect B and D.

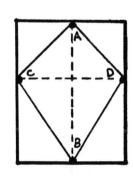

   Cut on the solid lines to make the kite shape.

4. Cut a piece of yarn 24" long and glue to the kite for a tail.

© 1992 by The Center for Applied Research in Education, Inc.

Teacher Time Saver

High Flier

5. Use paper from the wallpaper book to cut 6 rectangles 4" by 2". Use your ruler to draw straight lines from corner to corner.

6. Put a penny on the rectangle where the lines cross and trace around it.

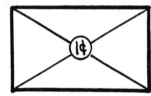

7. Cut out the bow shape and glue onto the kite string.

8. Decorate your kite anyway you wish.

SO BIG!

OBJECTIVE: Students will use centimeters to measure body parts.

MATERIALS: Yarn
Meter stick
Student Activity Sheet

PROCEDURE:
1. Cut three pieces of yarn (30cm, 100 cm, 150 cm) for the students to use.
2. Duplicate the Student Activity Sheet for each student.

TEACHER DIRECTIONS TO STUDENTS:
1. You will need to work in pairs for this center.
2. Use the yarn to measure the body parts and record on the Student Activity Sheet.

Make sure the students know how to use the string to measure. It's a good idea to practice before starting the center.

CONTENT HINT: Use with a unit about the body. You can make a great graph of the students height quickly by having the students lie down on a long 2 cm wide strip of paper and cut to fit the height of the student. They measure with the meter stick and put their name on it. Arrange the strips in order of height on a classroom wall!

So Big

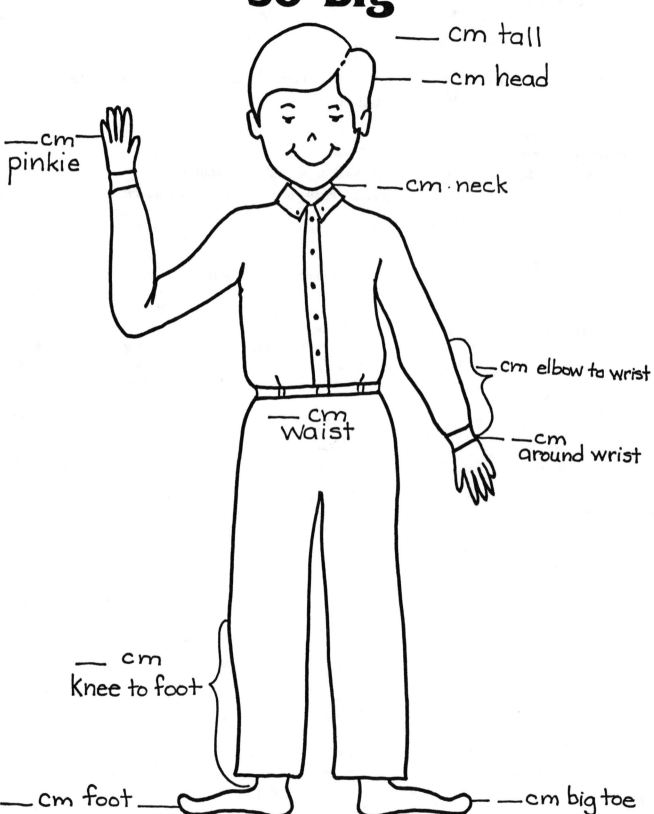

— cm tall

— cm head

— cm pinkie

— cm neck

— cm elbow to wrist

— cm waist

— cm around wrist

— cm knee to foot

— cm foot

— cm big toe

PLAY DOUGH

OBJECTIVE: Students will make play dough by measuring and following directions.

MATERIALS: Flour

Salt

Water

Oil

Food coloring (optional)

Large plastic bowl

Two measuring cups—label one dry and one water

One teaspoon

Wax paper

Cardboard

Teacher Time Saver

PROCEDURE:
1. Post the Teacher Time Saver.
2. Provide the materials listed above.
3. If you wish to use food coloring, give the directions to the students about care and use.

TEACHER DIRECTIONS TO STUDENTS:
1. Two students may work in this center.
2. Measure the dry ingredients in the measuring cup marked "dry," and the water in the cup marked "water."
3. Then tear off a piece of wax paper and roll and shape your favorite animal.
4. Put your animal on the cardboard to dry.

Ask parents or students to contribute to flour (a 5-pound bag is more than enough) and salt (7 or 8 boxes).

CONTENT HINT: Coordinate with a unit about animals. After the animals are dry, they can be painted with tempera paint.

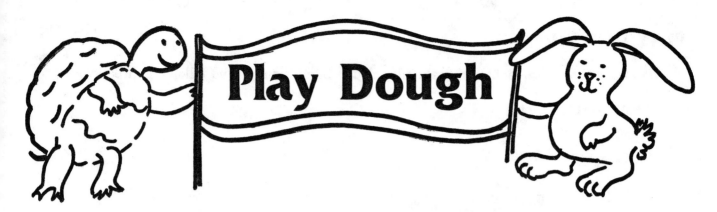

Play Dough

Use the large bowl to mix:

1 cup salt
1 cup flour
½ cup water
3 teaspoons oil

Mix with your hands until it is smooth. Give your friend half. On a piece of wax paper, make your favorite animal. Put your play dough on the cardboard to dry.

STEP ON THE SCALES

OBJECTIVE: Students will graph the weight of six classmates.

MATERIALS: Slips of paper with student weights

Crayons

Student Activity Sheet

PROCEDURE:
1. All students should weigh themselves on scales and write their name and weight on a slip of paper and fold.
2. Put the papers into a butter tub or other container.
3. Duplicate the Student Activity Sheet for each student.

If putting names on the paper is a problem for your class or you feel could be embarrassing, then ask them to make up a name of someone who is not in the room. You may even wish to omit the name and put a number on each card yourself.

TEACHER DIRECTIONS TO STUDENTS:
1. Draw out five pieces of paper from the tub.
2. Write the name and weight of each person on the graph.
3. Color in the graph to the nearest five pounds.
4. Answer the questions at the bottom of the graph.

CONTENT HINT: Use with a unit about healthy bodies. A large graph for the entire class can be made after the center is completed by all students.

Step on the Scales

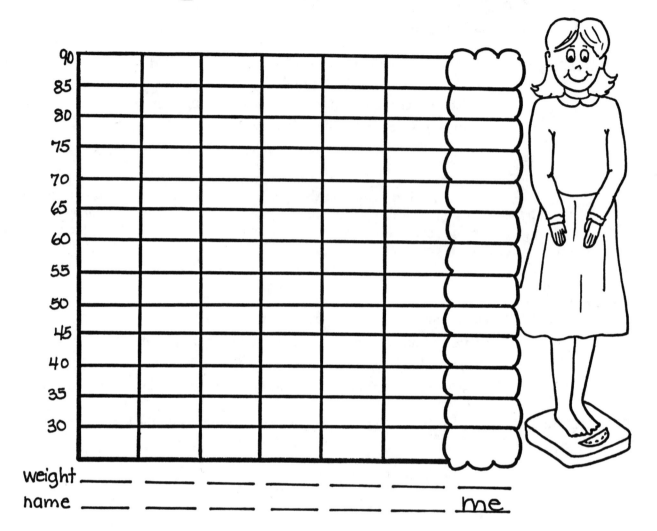

weight ____ ____ ____ ____ ____ ____
name ____ ____ ____ ____ ____ ____ me

Who weighed the most? _____
Who weighed the least? _____
How much more did the most weigh than the
   least? ____ lbs.
How much do you weigh? _____ lbs.
Do you weigh more or less than the heaviest person?___
How much more or less? ____ lbs.
How much will the least weigh if you add 15
   pounds? _____ lbs.

Geometry

RICE IS NICE!

OBJECTIVE: Students will demonstrate an understanding of geometric terms by using rice.

MATERIALS: Rice

Glue

Pencil

Ruler

Student Activity Sheets I, II and III

PROCEDURE:
1. Pour rice into a whipped topping tub for easy access.
2. Use a shoe box lid to catch excess rice.
3. Copy Student Activity Sheet onto colored copy paper if possible.

TEACHER DIRECTIONS TO STUDENTS:
1. Read the geometric definitions on the Student Activity Sheet.
2. Put glue where directed to do so and shake rice onto glue. Make sure you hold it over the lid to catch the excess rice.
3. Put your paper on the counter to dry.

 To make rice various colors, put 2 tablespoons of rubbing alcohol and a few drops of food coloring in a quart jar. Add rice and shake. Let dry. This looks good on white paper.

Rice is Nice!

Polygon: A closed shape with straight sides and corners.

Glue and rice the polygons.

Student Activity Sheet I

Rice is Nice!

Diagonals : Line segments connecting corners of polygons.

Make the diagonals. Glue and rice them.

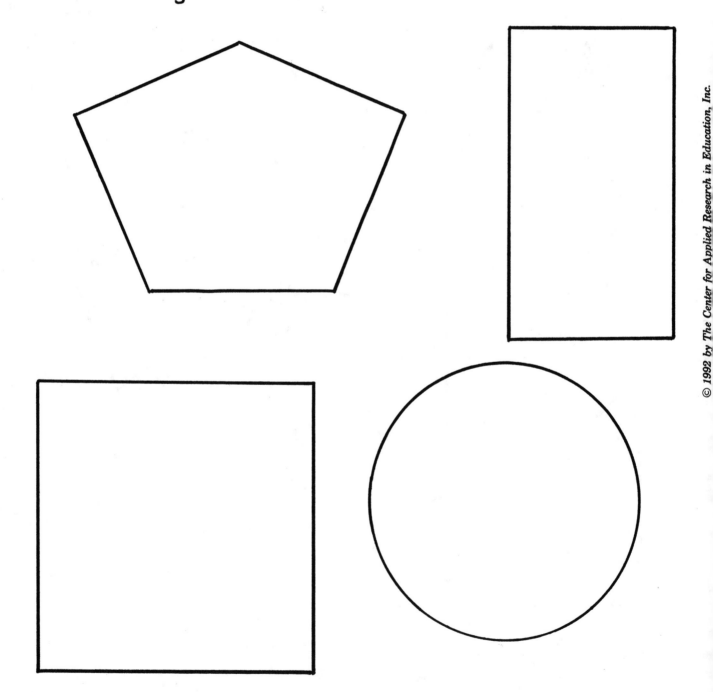

Student Activity Sheet II

Rice is Nice!

Line segment: A straight line with a beginning and ending point.

Glue and rice the line segments.

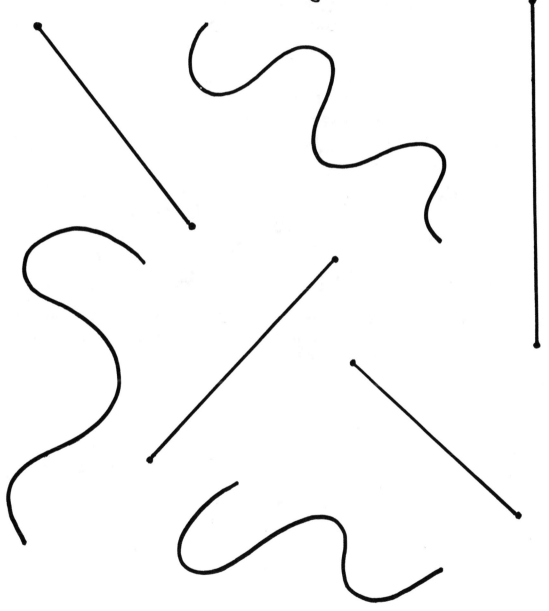

Student Activity Sheet III

FEED THE BIRDS

OBJECTIVE: Students will fashion geometric shapes from pipe cleaners, string them with oat cereal, and hang them for birds to eat in winter.

MATERIALS: 12″ pipe cleaners

One box oat cereal

Yarn

Teacher Time Saver

PROCEDURE:
1. Pour cereal into a box or plastic bowl for easy access.
2. Cut yarn into 6″ lengths.
3. Copy and laminate cards from the Teacher Time Saver.

TEACHER DIRECTIONS TO STUDENTS:
1. Choose two cards from the stack.
2. Make the shape and put the pieces of cereal on the pipe cleaner.
3. Tie the yarn on the shape for us to hang outside for the birds.

CONTENT HINT: Use with a Science unit about weather, winter, or seasons. Take the students outside to hang the bird feeders. Try to place them so that students can watch the birds from the classroom window.

 # Feed the Birds

Make a triangle.

Put six pieces of cereal on each side.

Make a rectangle.

Put eight pieces of cereal on the long sides. Put two pieces on the short sides.

Make a circle.

Put 16 pieces of cereal on the shape.

Make a square.

Put five pieces of cereal on each side.

Make a triangle.

Put seven pieces of cereal on each side.

Make a rectangle.

Put six pieces of cereal on the long sides and three pieces on the short sides.

Make a circle.

Put 20 pieces of cereal on the shape.

Make a square.

Put nine pieces of cereal on each side.

PIZZAZZ PIZZA

OBJECTIVE: Students will make a pizza by cutting out geometric shapes to form various toppings

MATERIALS: Brown, green, orange, and yellow construction paper

Crayons

Glue

Scissors

Student Activity Sheet

Teacher Time Saver

PROCEDURE:
1. Cut construction paper into $3'' \times 4\frac{1}{2}''$ pieces.
2. Duplicate one copy of Student Activity Sheet for each student.
3. Copy Teacher Time Saver and put in the center for students to follow directions.

TEACHER DIRECTIONS TO STUDENTS:
1. Make an interesting pizza by following the directions in the pizza center.
2. Cut out small geometric shapes in the colors that are written.
3. Use your crayons to color the sauce and crust before you begin.

 An alternative to using the Student Activity Sheet is to give the students large red circles to use as the pizza base.

CONTENT HINT: Use with a Health unit about foods or in a Social Studies unit dealing with ethnic groups.

Name _____ Date _____

Pizzazz Pizza

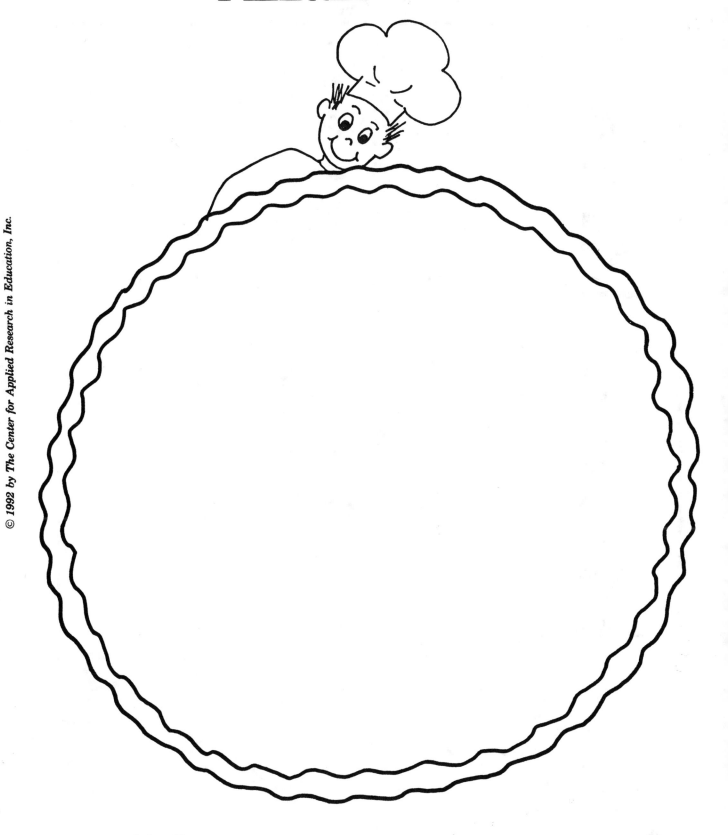

Student Activity Sheet

Pizzazz Pizza

Pizzazz Pizza

Pizza Sauce = Red

Pepperoni = Brown circles

Green Peppers = Green rectangles

Hamburger = Orange squares

Cheese = Yellow triangles

Crust = Tan

GEOMETRIC COLLAGE

OBJECTIVE: Students will make a collage from magazine pictures using two given geometric shapes.

MATERIALS: Colorful magazines
12" × 18" colored construction paper
Scissors
Glue
Teacher Time Saver I or II

PROCEDURE:
1. Collect a supply of magazines with many pictures.
2. Make copies of Teacher Time Saver I or II depending on the level of your group.

TEACHER DIRECTIONS TO STUDENTS:
1. Choose a color of construction paper for the background of your collage.
2. Take a card from the stack. It will tell you which two geometric shapes you need to look for in the magazines.
3. Cut out as many pictures as you need to fill your page and make a collage.
4. Glue your card onto the bottom of the collage and write your name.

CONTENT HINT: Use with a health unit about foods and cut out foods that fit that shape. Or use with a recreation unit and glue onto shapes of recreational equipment such as balls or kites.

Geometric Collage

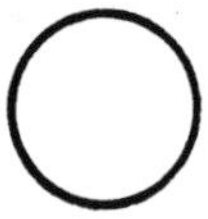

◯ circle

▢ square

Name _____

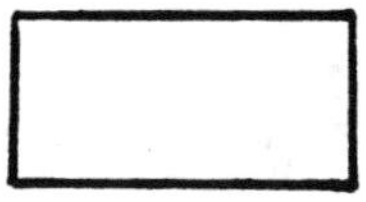

▭ rectangle

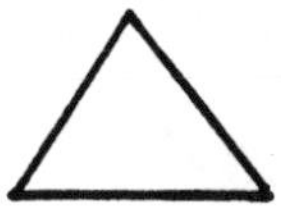

△ triangle

Name _____

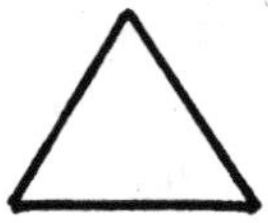

△ triangle

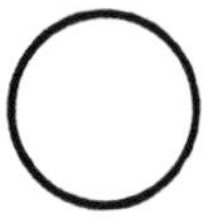

◯ circle

Name _____

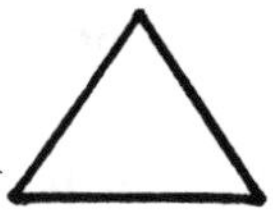

△ triangle

▢ square

Name _____

▭ rectangle

◯ circle

Name _____

▭ rectangle

▢ square

Name _____

Geometric Collage

sphere

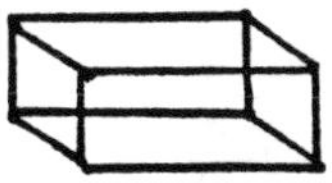

rectangular solid

Name _____

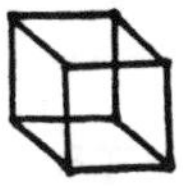

cube

cone

Name _____

cylinder

pyramid

Name _____

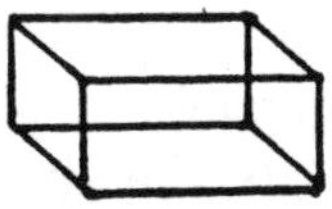

rectangular solid

pyramid

Name _____

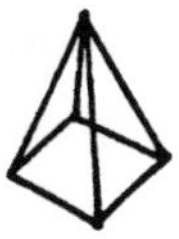

pyramid

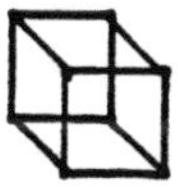

cube

Name _____

cone

sphere

Name _____

sphere

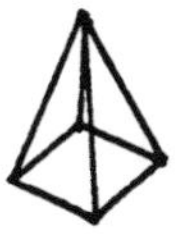

pyramid

Name _____

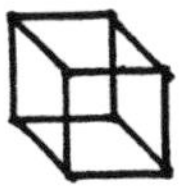

cube

cylinder

Name _____

SALTY SHAPES

OBJECTIVE: Students will trace geometric shapes and write the corresponding vocabulary in a salt tray and make the four basic geometric shapes on tagboard.

MATERIALS: One box of salt

One cookie sheet or box of similar size

Glue

Tagboard or sturdy paper

Teacher Time Saver

PROCEDURE:
1. Pour salt onto cookie sheet.
2. Duplicate Teacher Time Saver and cut out shapes to be used as patterns, or laminate and use for students to refer to when writing vocabulary. If you choose, you may make your own shape patterns from cardboard.

TEACHER DIRECTIONS TO STUDENTS:
1. Look at the pictures of the shapes. Make the shape in the salt tray with your finger. Write the shape word under the shape. Practice several times.
2. Trace and cut out each of the geometric shapes and write the shape word on one side and your initials on the other.
3. Trace each shape with glue and sprinkle with salt. Put them on the counter to dry.

 You may wish to have your students make mobiles of their shapes. Simply make a hole in each shape and tie with a yarn string. Suspend strings from a coat hanger.

CONTENT HINT: Use with the study of a holiday. Use seasonal colors of construction paper and substitute glitter for the trimming of the shapes.

Salty Shapes

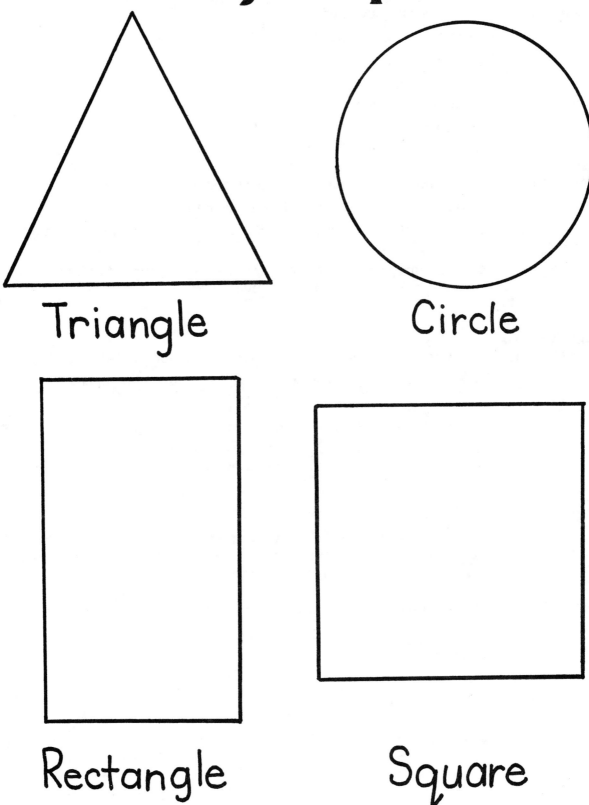

Triangle

Circle

Rectangle

Square

MELVIN OR MILLIE MONSTER!

OBJECTIVE: Students will use geometric vocabulary, trace geometric shapes, and use those shapes to create a picture

MATERIALS: Colored construction paper
Geometric shapes to trace
Scissors
Glue
12″ × 18″ manila paper
Box of scraps, sequins, glitter, buttons
Cards from Teacher Time Saver

PROCEDURE:
1. Duplicate the Teacher Time Saver and cut apart the cards.
2. Cut various sizes of colored construction paper.
3. Make patterns for large and small shapes—squares, circles, triangles, and rectangles.
4. Make sure you have interesting materials in your "scrap box" such as sequins, foil, buttons, rick-rack, and glitter.

TEACHER DIRECTIONS TO STUDENTS:
1. Choose a card and follow the directions to trace and cut out shapes.
2. Put the shapes together to make a Melvin or Millie Monster.
3. Glue the monster onto the manila paper.
4. You may add extra pizzazz to your monster by using materials in the scrap box.
5. Put your monster on the bulletin board.

 You may wish to make a background for a bulletin board and have the students pin their monsters onto it instead of gluing them onto manila paper. Create your own Monsterville!

CONTENT HINT: Use when reading various books about Monsters or wild and scary creatures.

Melvin or Millie Monster

Trace and cut:

2 small rectangles
3 large circles
4 small triangles
1 large triangle
6 small squares

Trace and cut:

1 large square
3 large circles
7 small triangles
2 small squares
8 small rectangles

Trace and cut:

4 small circles
9 small rectangles
2 large triangles
1 large rectangle
3 small squares

Trace and cut:

2 small rectangles
1 large triangle
4 large circles
6 small squares
5 small triangles

Trace and cut:

5 large triangles
3 small rectangles
8 small circles
1 large circles
2 small squares

Trace and cut:

2 large triangles
9 small squares
7 small circles
4 large rectangles
1 large circle

Trace and cut:

3 small triangles
5 large circles
1 large square
9 small squares
2 large rectangles

Trace and cut:

6 small rectangles
7 large triangles
4 small circles
1 large rectangle
3 small squares

Teacher Time Saver

Shapely Graph

OBJECTIVE: Students will use geometric shapes to make a graph and then interpret the information on the graph.

MATERIALS: Crayons
Teacher Time Saver
Student Activity Sheet
Clear self-stick vinyl

PROCEDURE:
1. Copy and laminate the Teacher Time Saver. Cut apart.
2. Duplicate a Student Activity Sheet for each student.

TEACHER DIRECTIONS TO STUDENTS:
1. Take a card from the stack.
2. Follow the directions to fill out your graph on the Student Activity Sheet.
3. Put the card number in the circle on your Student Activity Sheet.

 It is helpful to do a large graph with the class using actual shapes to fill in the spaces. After the students complete their graphs, display around the large class graph.

Shapely Graph

Name _____

Date _____

	Rectangle	Circle	Square	Triangle
8				
7				
6				
5				
4				
3				
2				
1				

Which shape did you have the most?_____

Which shape did you have the least?_____

Circles and triangles together make how many?_____

Did you have more rectangles or squares?_____

Compare your graph with a friend's graph. Who has more triangles?_____ circles?_____

Student Activity Sheet

Shapely Graph

Use Red ①	Use Green ②
6 rectangles 3 circles 2 squares 4 triangles	5 rectangles 1 circle 8 squares 6 triangles

Use Purple ③	Use Orange ④
4 rectangles 2 circles 7 squares 3 triangles	5 rectangles 4 circles 8 squares 2 triangles

Use any Color ⑤	Use Blue ⑥
8 rectangles 3 circles 1 square 4 triangles	7 rectangles 1 circle 6 squares 2 triangles

Use Red or Yellow ⑦	Use Black or Pink ⑧
4 rectangles 1 circle 5 squares 3 triangles	6 rectangles 4 circles 1 square 2 triangles

Use any Color ⑨	Use Green and Purple ⑩
7 rectangles 1 circle 5 square 2 triangles	6 rectangles 3 circles 8 squares 2 triangles

Use Orange and Blue ⑪	Use Red and Brown ⑫
4 rectangles 8 circles 1 square 3 triangles	5 rectangles 3 circles 5 squares 1 triangle

Fractions

SEASONAL SYMMETRY

OBJECTIVE: Students will be able to divide seasonal shapes in half and use the term "symmetrical."

MATERIALS: 9″ × 12″ black construction paper
Seasonal shape patterns
Colored construction paper
Student activity sheet
Teacher time saver

PROCEDURE: 1. Trace pattern you wish to use onto cardboard

2. Discuss the terms symmetrical and symmetry with students. Make sure they understand that to be symmetrical both sides or halves of an object must be identical.

3. Demonstrate how to fold a black piece of paper in half and draw half a tree. Cut it out and unfold it to show symmetry.

TEACHER DIRECTIONS TO STUDENTS:

1. Draw and cut out a black symmetrical tree. Glue it onto the answer sheet.

2. Use the "half" shape for the season to trace and cut out decorations for the tree. Remember the straight edge must be on the fold.

Example:

Valentines   Pumpkins   Flowers

CONTENT HINT: *Science* or *Social Studies*

Use with seasons or holiday unit.

Name _____ Date _____

"Symmetre-e-e"

Symmetry Patterns

$\frac{1}{2}$ Of A Whole Is $\frac{1}{2}$

OBJECTIVE: Students will be able to cut geometric shapes in half and label each half with the fraction $\frac{1}{2}$.

MATERIALS: Geometric patterns

Colored construction paper

Crayons

Student activity sheet

Teacher time saver

PROCEDURE:
1. Trace the provided shapes onto tag or heavy paper and cut out for students to use as patterns.
2. Reproduce the Center Activity Sheet.

TEACHER DIRECTIONS TO STUDENTS:
1. Trace each of the shapes and cut in half.
2. Write the number $\frac{1}{2}$ on each piece.
3. Paste the pieces on your paper to make a picture.
4. Use your crayons to finish the picture.

CONTENT HINT: *Science*

Correlate with animal or plant unit.

$$\frac{1}{2} \text{---} \frac{1}{2} \text{---} \frac{1}{2} \text{---} \frac{1}{2}$$

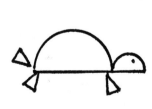

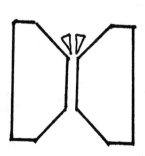

Student Activity Sheet

Patterns

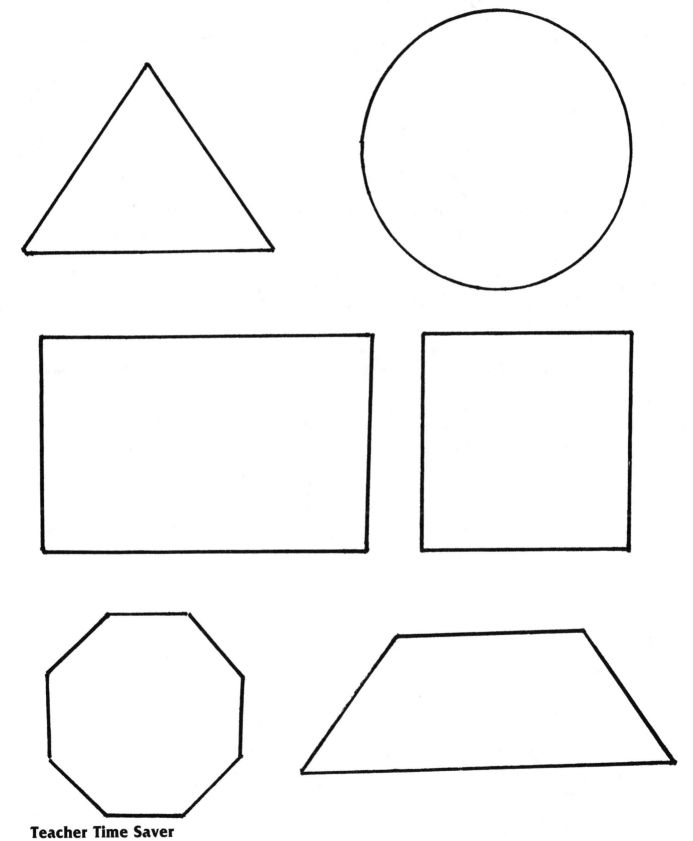

Teacher Time Saver

SPARKLING THIRDS MOBILE

OBJECTIVE: Students will demonstrate knowledge of thirds by making their own mobile.

MATERIALS: Colored construction paper.

Patterns

Glitter

Glue

Yarn

Clothes hanger or dowel

Hole punch

Scissors, ruler

Teacher time saver pages

PROCEDURE:
1. Trace the provided shapes onto cardboard for patterns.
2. Clip notches for students to draw lines when they trace the patterns.

TEACHER DIRECTIONS TO STUDENTS:
1. Trace the patterns onto your choice of construction paper.
2. Draw the lines to show thirds on each shape.
3. Glue and glitter $\frac{1}{3}$ of each shape.
4. Punch a hole for yarn and hang the shapes from the dowel for your mobile.

CONTENT HINT: *Social Studies*
Use at Christmas with a unit about holidays.

Sparkling Thirds Mobile Patterns

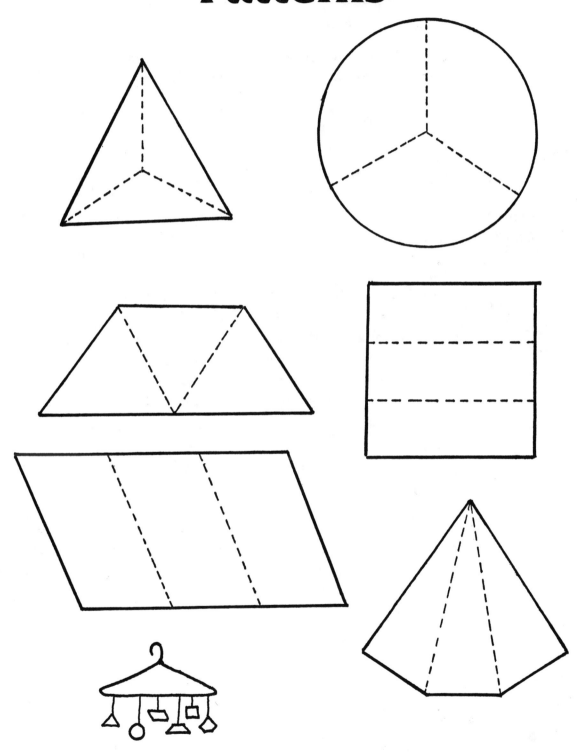

SPILL AND DRAW

OBJECTIVE: Students will be able to divide a set number of beans into halves, thirds, and fourths.

MATERIALS: Three-film canisters
43 large lima beans
Crayons and pencil
Student activity sheet

PROCEDURE: In one film canister put 16 beans and label $\frac{1}{2}$, in another canister put 15 beans and label $\frac{1}{3}$, and in the third canister put 12 beans and label $\frac{1}{4}$.

TEACHER DIRECTIONS TO STUDENTS:

1. On your answer sheet you will see $\frac{1}{2}$, $\frac{1}{3}$, and $\frac{1}{4}$. Use only one canister at a time for this center.

2. Open the canister with $\frac{1}{2}$ on it. Spill the beans so that half the beans are on each boxed marked $\frac{1}{2}$.

3. Trace each bean and return beans to the canister.

4. Spill the canister of beans marked $\frac{1}{3}$ so that you have the same amount in each of the three boxes marked $\frac{1}{3}$.

5. Trace each bean and return them to the canister.

6. Spill the beans in the canister marked $\frac{1}{6}$ and put the same amount in each boxed marked $\frac{1}{4}$.

7. Trace each bean and return them to the canister.

9. Color the beans.

This activity can be further extended by having the students write the number of beans in each box, by having them write the fractional part before reduction, i.e., $\frac{8}{16}, \frac{8}{16} - \frac{5}{15}, \frac{5}{15}, \frac{5}{15}$ etc., or having them color each fractional box a different color (i.e., for the fourths use red for one box, blue for the second, green for the third, and yellow for the fourth).

CONTENT HINT: *Science*
Use when you study plants or seeds.

Spill and Draw

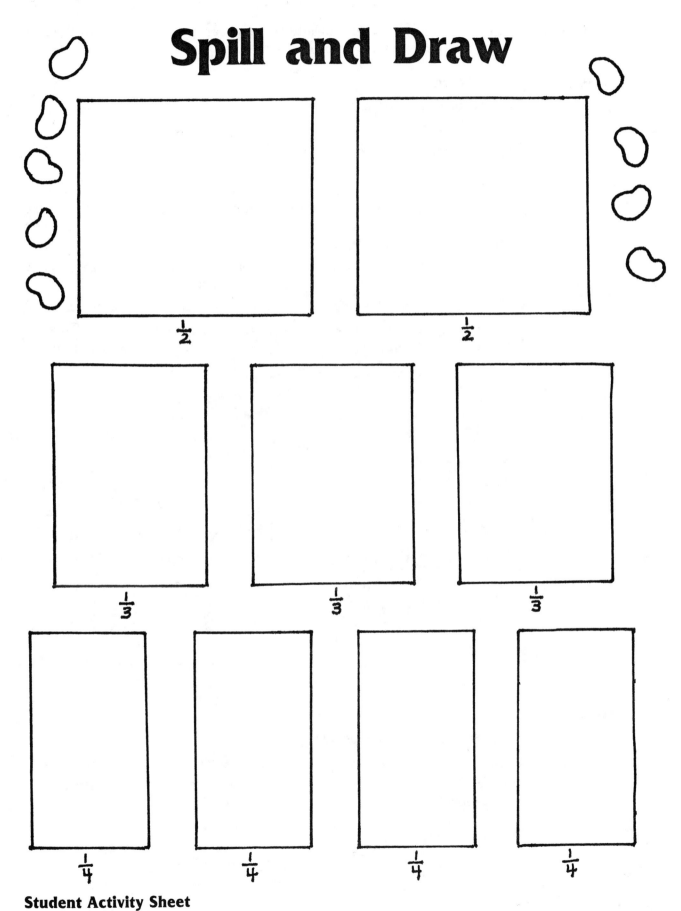

$\frac{1}{2}$ $\frac{1}{2}$

$\frac{1}{3}$ $\frac{1}{3}$ $\frac{1}{3}$

$\frac{1}{4}$ $\frac{1}{4}$ $\frac{1}{4}$ $\frac{1}{4}$

© 1992 by The Center for Applied Research in Education, Inc.

Student Activity Sheet

JOE'S GRILL

OBJECTIVE: Students will be able to put foods together to form a whole and tell the fractional parts they were cut into.

MATERIALS: Bulletin board

Magazine or drawn pictures of food

Five paper plates

Student activity sheet

Clear self-stick vinyl

PROCEDURE:
1. Cut out foods from a magazine that would be found in a grill (i.e., hot dog, hamburger, pizza, club sandwich, milk shake, soda, pickle, pie, cake, cookie, etc.). Then cut each into halves, thirds, or fourths.

   You may wish to draw these or have a parent volunteer to make them for you. Laminating would make this a durable center.

2. Enlarge and color the picture of Joe and his grill for your bulletin board.

3. Cut two paper plates in half and glue onto the three whole ones. This will make a pocket. On them write $\frac{1}{2}$, $\frac{1}{3}$, $\frac{1}{4}$ and staple onto the bulletin board.

TEACHER DIRECTIONS TO STUDENTS:
1. Take the food pictures out of the bag.
2. Put the puzzle pieces together.
3. Put them in the plate pocket that shows the fractional parts they are cut into.
4. On your answer sheet draw the thing you like that was cut in halves, thirds, and fourths.

CONTENT HINT: *Health* and *Social Studies*

Use with unit about foods, nutrition, or community workers.

Joe's Grill

Name _____

Date _____

I like the foods that were cut into these fractional parts.

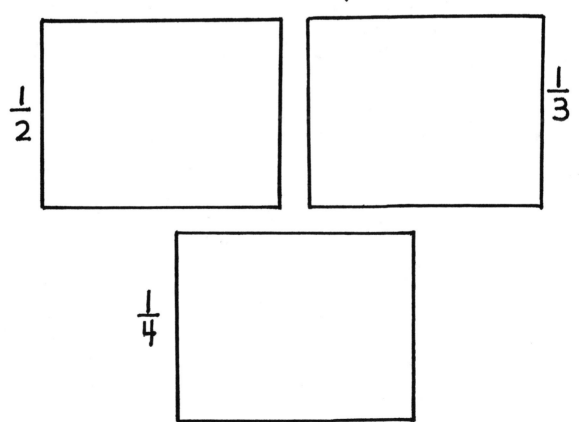

$\frac{1}{2}$

$\frac{1}{3}$

$\frac{1}{4}$

Student Activity Sheet

COLORED RICE

OBJECTIVE: Students will be able to measure and record the amount of rice in a measuring cup.

MATERIALS: Dish pan or similar size container
5 lb. (approx.) of rice
Large margarine tub with lid
Food coloring
Rubbing alcohol
Measuring cup
Student activity sheet

PROCEDURE:
1. Put one tablespoon of rubbing alcohol and a few drops of food coloring into a margarine tub and shake. Add two cups of rice and shake again. This will make colored rice. You may want to make several different colors of rice and then mix them together in the dish pan.
2. Put pan of rice and measuring cup in the center.

TEACHER DIRECTIONS TO STUDENTS:
1. Look at the activity page to see how much rice to measure.
2. Measure the rice.
3. Color that amount of rice in the measuring cup.

Name _____ **Date** _____

Colored Rice

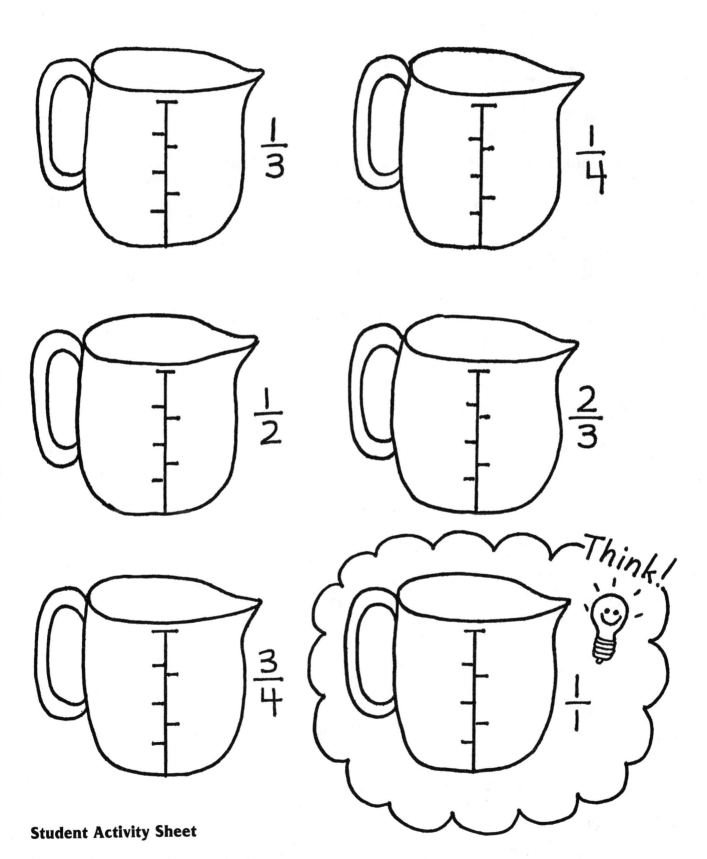

Student Activity Sheet

SPIN A FRACTION

OBJECTIVE: Students will be able to recognize and reproduce as fraction a circle using a protractor to draw the circles.

MATERIALS: Protractor

Ruler

Markers or crayons

Spinner

Student activity sheet

Teacher time saver

PROCEDURE:
1. Reproduce the provided spinner and glue onto cardboard for durability. Make an arrow from tagboard and attach with a large brad.
2. Put protractor, ruler, and markers in a can or box for use in the center.

TEACHER DIRECTIONS TO STUDENTS:
1. Draw four circles on the answer sheet using the protractor.
2. Spin the spinner and write the fraction on the line under the circle.
3. Use the ruler to draw the fractional shape. Color the fractions.

Name _____ Date _____

Spin a Fraction

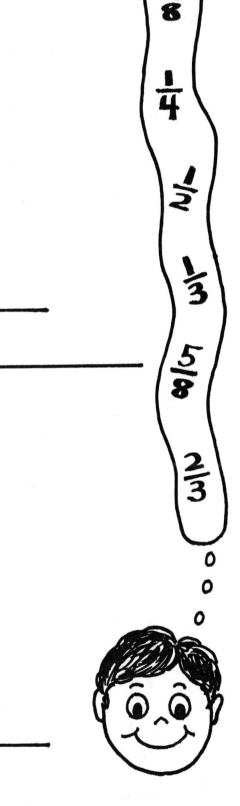

_____   _____

_____   _____

Student Activity Sheet

© 1992 by The Center for Applied Research in Education, Inc.

Spinners

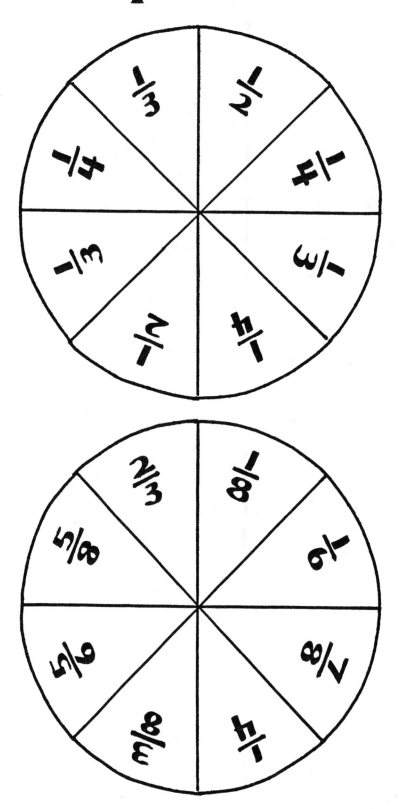

ADD A BEAD

OBJECTIVE: Students will be able to demonstrate knowledge of the fraction $\frac{1}{3}$ by making a necklace.

MATERIALS: Sandwich bag

Three varieties of pasta with holes

Yarn cut into 18″ or 20″ strips

[Styrofoam pieces, needle, and string can be substituted for pasta and yarn]

PROCEDURE: *Optional:* Using food coloring, dye each type of pasta a different color.

1. Put each type of pasta in a separate container.

2. Dipping the ends of the yarn into glue and allowing to dry overnight makes stringing easy.

3. On small pieces of paper write a few numbers that are divisible by three and put into sandwich baggie.

TEACHER DIRECTIONS TO STUDENTS:

1. Choose a number from the Baggie.

2. Divide the number by three.

3. Lay out your noodles so that you have $\frac{1}{3}$ of each of the three kinds of pasta.

4. Show your teacher.

5. Now string the pasta into a necklace to take home.

ALTERNATE SUGGESTION: Fractions that suit your class needs can be used—fourths, fifths, etc. Provide slips of paper that say things like / Make $\frac{2}{6}$ green, $\frac{1}{6}$ yellow, and $\frac{3}{6}$ red / (if you use colored pastas).

CONTENT HINT: *Social Studies*

Correlate with an Indian unit.

A TISKET, A TASKET

OBJECTIVE: Students will be able to graph eggs and then write the fraction that was colored.

MATERIALS: Basket
Ten plastic eggs
Strips of paper with directions
Crayons
Student activity sheet
Teacher time saver

PROCEDURE:
1. Cut strips of paper from teacher time saver.
2. Put one strip into each egg.
3. Put eggs in the basket.

TEACHER DIRECTIONS TO STUDENTS:
1. Choose an egg from the basket.
2. Follow the directions on the slip of paper found in the egg.
3. Record your answers on the answer graph.

CONTENT HINT: *Social Studies*
Correlate with Spring unit.

A Tisket, A Tasket Graph

| rabbits | eggs | chicks | daffodils |

1. What fraction of the chicks were colored? _____
2. What fraction of the eggs were colored? _____
3. What fraction of the daffodils were colored? _____
4. What fraction of the rabbits were colored? _____
5. Write the fractions for the rabbits and chicks colored and circle the larger fraction.

Student Activity Sheet   Name _____   Date _____

Color: 3 rabbits, 5 eggs, 2 chicks, 8 daffodils

Color: 2 rabbits, 9 eggs, 6 chicks, 3 daffodils

Color: 5 rabbits, 7 eggs, 1 chick, 10 daffodils

Color: 3 rabbits, 1 egg, 8 chicks, 11 daffodils

Color: 9 rabbits, 2 eggs, 6 chicks, 2 daffodils

Color: 8 rabbits, 4 eggs, 12 chicks, 3 daffodils

Color: 1 rabbit, 5 eggs, 9 chicks, 6 daffodils

Color: 2 rabbits, 10 eggs, 7 chicks, 4 daffodils

* Super Slip
Color: $\frac{1}{3}$ of the rabbits, $\frac{1}{4}$ eggs, $\frac{1}{2}$ chicks, $\frac{1}{3}$ daffodils

* Super Slip
Color: $\frac{2}{4}$ of the rabbits, $\frac{1}{2}$ eggs, $\frac{2}{3}$ chicks, $\frac{1}{4}$ daffodils

© 1992 by The Center for Applied Research in Education, Inc.

Addition and Subtraction to 19

BUNNY HOP

OBJECTIVE: Students will be able to subtract from 19 or less.

MATERIALS: Nine 3″ × 12″ strips of paper   Margarine tub (large)
Bunny stamp   Student Activity Sheet
Ink pad   11 small squares of paper (2″ × 2″)

PROCEDURE:
1. On 11 small squares of paper, print the numbers 0 to 11 (one number on each piece).
2. On the 9 pieces of 3″ × 12″ paper, stamp 11 to 19 bunnies and write the amount.

   Example:

3. Cut a hole in the side of the margarine tub.

   Example:

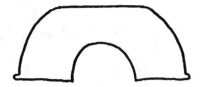

4. Duplicate Student Activity Sheet.

TEACHER DIRECTIONS TO STUDENTS:
1. Bunnies like to hide in their hole. Choose a card from the small stack and read the number.
2. Have that many bunnies go to their hole by placing the hole (margarine tub) over them.
3. Count to see how many are left.
4. Do the same thing with each set of bunnies and count how many are left.
5. Choose another card and repeat.
6. When you have practiced as much as you want, use the bunny hole to do the Student Activity Sheet.

CONTENT HINT: *Science*

Use with unit on animals. This is also a good time to coordinate with P.E. by teaching the Bunny Hop. Don't forget to read *Peter Rabbit* by Beatrix Potter for Literature.

© 1992 by The Center for Applied Research in Education, Inc.

Bunny Hop

12 − 4 = □

14 − 7 = □

17 − 9 = □

13 − 6 = □

Student Activity Sheet

Name _____ Date _____

HOW OLD ARE YOU?

OBJECTIVE: Students will add or subtract using candles.

MATERIALS: 38 candles
Round box
Two Ziplock Baggies
Yellow construction paper (6″ × 5″ scrap)
Teacher Time Saver
Student Activity Sheet
Clear self-stick vinyl

PROCEDURE:
1. Decorate a round box to look like a birthday cake. (A large oatmeal box cut in half works fine.)
2. Poke nineteen holes in the top of the cake (box). Make sure the candles fit snugly into them.
3. Put nineteen candles into one baggie.
4. Use yellow paper to make nineteen flames and glue onto the other candles and put into a baggie.
5. Duplicate Teacher Time Saver and cut apart cards. (Laminate for durability.)
6. Duplicate Student Activity Sheet for each child.

TEACHER DIRECTIONS TO STUDENTS:
1. Choose a number sentence card.
2. Put candles on the cake to show the problem.

   Example: If you choose $\boxed{15 - 3}$, put 15 "flaming" candles on the cake. Take out three and replace them with three "unlit" candles. Count those that are still "flaming."
3. Do each card in the stack. Some will be add and some subtract.
4. Do the Student Activity Sheet by drawing your candles to show the problem.

CONTENT HINT: *Social Studies*

Use with unit about Home and Family Celebrations.

Name _____ Date _____

How Old Are You?

Draw candles to show the problem.
Put flames on those that stay lit.

4 + 2

11 - 3

19 - 13

14 - 6

12 + 3

Student Activity Sheet

How Old Are You?

13-4	17-6	10+3
15+2	9+8	19-10
7+11	12-8	13+4
18-3	8+8	15-9
6+9	14-8	12+7
11-3	15+4	16-6
9+9	12-7	15-3

TOSS AND RECORD

OBJECTIVE: Students will be able to subtract from 19 or less by using a beanbag floor game.

MATERIALS: Two large pieces of bulletin board paper (different colors), butcher paper, or tag board (ex.: one red and one yellow)

Two beanbags

Beans or other counters to manipulate

Student Activity Sheet

Clear self-stick vinyl

PROCEDURE: 1. On the red (36″ × 26″) piece of brightly colored bulletin board paper, make nine blocks and write the numerals 11 through 19 in random order. On the yellow piece write 9 numerals 0 to 10. (Laminating helps preserve these pages!)

Example:

11	19	13
14	17	18
15	12	16

6	1	3
8	5	7
2	4	9

2. Supply two beanbags and counters, such as beans, for the students who need or want to use manipulatives to answer the subtraction problem.

3. Copy the Student Activity Sheet for each student.

TEACHER DIRECTIONS TO STUDENTS:

1. Put the two number charts on the floor.

2. Toss a beanbag on the red chart and record the large numeral on the Student Activity Sheet. Toss a beanbag on the yellow chart and record that numeral. Subtract.

3. You may do the problems mentally or use manipulatives to derive the answer.

4. Don't forget to put in the minus and equal signs.

 This is a good activity to use for cooperative learning or paired teaching. One child could record while the other tosses the beanbag and then exchange places. Working together makes this a lot of fun for the students while they are learning.

Toss and Record

5	4	2
3	1	9
6	7	8

11	15	18
12	17	13
19	14	16

Student Activity Sheet

HIGH ROLLERS

OBJECTIVE: Students will be able to create and answer a subtraction problem by using dice and an animal stamp.

MATERIALS: Two dice
Cute animal stamp
Ink pad
Pencil
Strips of paper large enough to accommodate 12 animal
Stamps in a row
Stapler

PROCEDURE:
1. Cut enough strips of paper for each child to have six.
2. Provide two dice.
3. Put animal stamp and ink pad in the center.
4. Duplicate Student Activity Sheet.

 If you are studying a particular unit, provide a stamp to coordinate with that unit.

TEACHER DIRECTIONS TO STUDENTS:
1. Roll two dice and count the dots.
2. Stamp that many animals in a row on one strip of paper.
3. Roll one die and count the dots.
4. Cross out that many animals.
5. Write the number story on the paper.
6. You may use six strips of paper.
7. Staple them to the Student Activity Sheet.
8. Use one die to subtract the animals on the Student Activity Sheet.
9. Write the number story.

High Rollers

Roll one die. Cross out that number of animals. Write the number story.

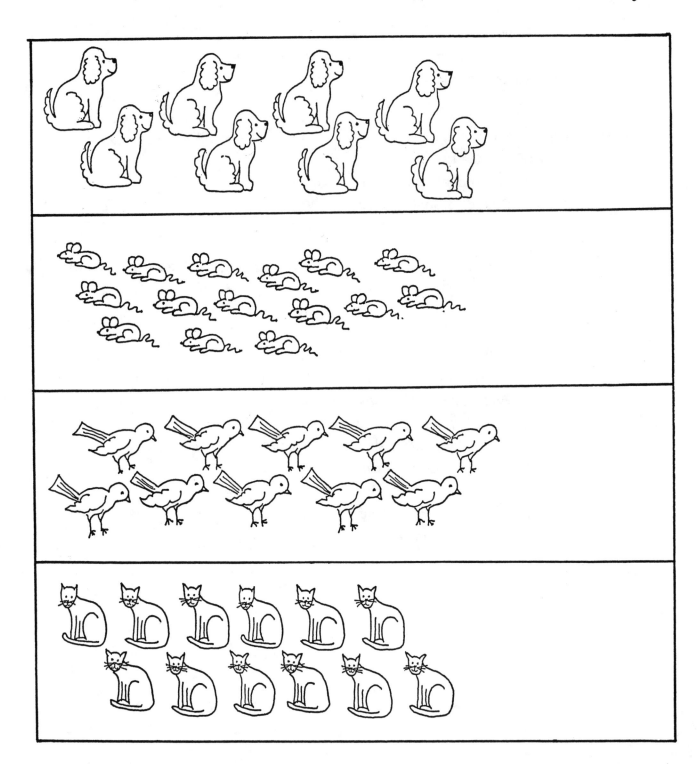

FRUITS AND VEGGIES

OBJECTIVE: Students will be able to choose a set of fruits or vegetables, draw a card with a number on it from a stack, and produce a subtraction fact.

MATERIALS: Teacher Time Saver pages

Pencil

Colored pencils or crayons

Paper clips

PROCEDURE:
1. Reproduce enough of Teacher Time Saver I so that each student can do five problems (half as many as you have students) and cut apart.
2. Reproduce Teacher Time Saver II, mount onto colored construction paper, and cut apart to make a stack of cards.
3. Provide a can of colored pencils or crayons.
4. Have paper clips handy.

TEACHER DIRECTIONS TO STUDENTS:
1. Choose five vegetable or fruit cards that you want to make subtraction facts about.
2. Make sure all number cards are face down in a pile.
3. Draw or take the top card.
4. Choose one of the vegetable/fruit cards and cross out (X) that many, and write the subtraction fact.

Example:

$$14 - 8 = 6$$

5. You may use the colored pencils to color those fruits or vegetables that are left.
6. Put the number cards on the bottom of the pile when you are finished.
7. Put your name on the back of each fruit or vegetable card.
8. Paper clip your five cards together to give to your teacher.

CONTENT HINT: *Health/Nutrition*

Use when studying foods or food groups.

Fruits and Veggies

Fruits and Veggies

5	4	7	8	4	4	6	9
7	5	9	5	9	9	8	7
9	4	6	8	5	7	4	6
6	7	4	9	6	8	8	5

Teacher Time Saver II

MONSTER MUNCH

OBJECTIVE: Students will add and subtract to nineteen using oat cereal.

MATERIALS: Paper lunch bag
Box oat cereal
Student Activity Sheet
Teacher Time Saver

PROCEDURE:
1. Make a copy of the Monster on the Teacher Time Saver, color, cut it out, and glue onto the lunch bag.
2. Put oat cereal into the bag.
3. Duplicate Student Activity Sheet for each student.

TEACHER DIRECTIONS TO STUDENTS:
1. Take enough cereal from the monster's bag to cover the cereal spaces on the first problems on your page.
2. Look at the sign to tell whether to add or subtract. If it is a minus you may eat the cereal you take away.
3. Use the same cereal as long as you can. You may get more if you need to.
4. When you finish, you may eat all the cereal that is left on your paper.

CONTENT HINT: *Social Studies*

Use with a unit about Halloween.

Literature

Coordinate with a story about monsters, goblins, etc.

Monster Munch

Put cereal on the shapes. Watch your signs and write the answers. You may eat the ones you subtract.

⊙⊙⊙⊙ + ⊙⊙⊙ ⊙⊙⊙⊙ ⊙⊙⊙ □	⊙⊙⊙⊙⊙ ⊙⊙⊙⊙⊙ − 3 ⊙⊙⊙⊙⊙ □
⊙⊙⊙ ⊙⊙⊙⊙ ⊙⊙⊙ + ⊙⊙⊙⊙ ⊙⊙⊙ □	⊙⊙⊙⊙⊙ ⊙⊙⊙⊙⊙ + ⊙ ⊙⊙⊙⊙⊙ ⊙ □
⊙⊙⊙⊙⊙ ⊙⊙⊙⊙⊙ − 10 ⊙⊙⊙⊙ □	⊙⊙⊙⊙ ⊙⊙⊙⊙ − 8 ⊙⊙⊙⊙ □
⊙⊙⊙⊙⊙⊙ ⊙⊙⊙⊙⊙ + ⊙⊙ ⊙⊙⊙⊙ ⊙ □	⊙⊙⊙⊙⊙ ⊙⊙⊙⊙ − 9 ⊙⊙⊙⊙ □
⊙⊙⊙⊙⊙⊙ ⊙⊙⊙⊙⊙⊙ − 13 ⊙⊙⊙⊙⊙⊙ □	⊙⊙⊙ ⊙⊙⊙ ⊙⊙⊙ + ⊙⊙⊙ ⊙⊙⊙ ⊙⊙ □

Teacher Time Saver

CATERWIGGLE   ☆☆☆

OBJECTIVE: Students will construct a caterpillar by using subtraction facts.

MATERIALS: Cardboard egg carton bottoms, one per child   Butter tub
Various colors of tempera paint   Wiggle eyes
Pipe cleaners   Teacher Time Saver

PROCEDURE:
1. Cut egg carton bottoms onto six strips. (Use a basket or box to hold all the pieces.)
2. Supply green paint for caterpillar.
3. You need orange, purple, red, or black paint for spots.
4. Cut pipe cleaners into fourths for legs.
5. Make several copies of Teacher Time Saver and cut apart. Put in a butter tub.
6. Make a model of the project. Show it while you explain the project.

TEACHER DIRECTIONS TO STUDENTS:
1. Draw three cards from the stack in the butter tub to start your caterpillar.
2. On one card, circle B for body.
   On one card, circle L for legs.
   One one card, circle S for spots.
3. Answer each subtraction problem to see how many parts you need.
   Example:

$$13 - 5 = \boxed{8}$$
   Ⓑ L S

This card tells you to give your caterpillar eight humps. Connect eight egg cartons humps together and paint with green tempera.

$$6 - 1 = \boxed{5}$$
   B Ⓛ S

On your second card where you circled L. you need to put five pipe cleaner legs.

$$11 - 3 = \boxed{8}$$
   B L Ⓢ

On the third card where you circled S, you need to choose red, orange, or purple paint to paint eight spots on your caterpillar.

4. When your caterpillar is dry, glue on two wiggle eyes and stick in two pipe cleaner antennae.
5. Staple all three cards together, put your name on them, and put with your "caterwiggle."

Caterwiggle

$12 - 4 = \square$ B L S	$9 - 2 = \square$ B L S	$14 - 7 = \square$ B L S
$8 - 1 = \square$ B L S	$15 - 9 = \square$ B L S	$10 - 3 = \square$ B L S
$17 - 8 = \square$ B L S	$7 - 9 = \square$ B L S	$19 - 7 = \square$ B L S
$11 - 3 = \square$ B L S	$6 - 1 = \square$ B L S	$13 - 5 = \square$ B L S
$5 - 0 = \square$ B L S	$18 - 9 = \square$ B L S	$16 - 4 = \square$ B L S
$16 - 6 = \square$ B L S	$14 - 5 = \square$ B L S	$12 - 2 = \square$ B L S

Teacher Time Saver

LOST TEETH

OBJECTIVE: Students will use subtraction to answer questions about a lost tooth graph.

MATERIALS: Pencil
Crayons or colored pencils
Student Activity Sheet

PROCEDURE: Make a copy of the Student Activity Sheet for each child.

TEACHER DIRECTIONS TO STUDENTS:
1. Interview five classmates to see how many teeth they have lost.
2. Write their name and fill in the graph to show the number of lost teeth.
3. Answer the questions at the bottom of the graph.

This can also be a home project where the child interviews family members or people outside of class.

CONTENT HINT: Use with a unit on Dental Health.

Lost Teeth

Interview 5 people and fill in the graph. Answer the questions.

12				
11				
10				
9				
8				
7				
6				
5				
4				
3				
2				
1				

name   name   name   name   name

1. Who lost the most teeth? _____
2. Who lost the fewest teeth? _____
3. Who lost more teeth than you? _____
   How many more? _____
4. Who lost fewer teeth than you? _____
   How many more did you lose? _____
5. How many teeth did the girls lose? _____
6. How many teeth did the boys lose? _____
7. Who lost more teeth — boys or girls? _____
   How many more teeth? _____

Student Activity Sheet   **Name** _____ **Date** _____

Math Centers

HOW TO USE

Instant monthly math centers are quick and easy to make and can be used year after year—a real time saver!

Duplicate as many of the large monthly designs as you will need for the center. The heavier the paper, the more durable the center will be. Then duplicate as many small pieces that coordinate with the large pieces as you need.

After each large piece has been colored and numbered, laminate and staple a baggie to the bottom. Write number combinations on the small pieces and laminate. The center can be stapled onto a bulletin board, clipped on the chalkboard with magnets, or with clips attached to a wall. If you prefer, you may attach the large pieces to boxes or coffee cans rather than stapling them onto the sandwich bags.

Let's try September, for example. If you are working on addition to five, you would reproduce five schoolhouses and twenty apples. Write a number on each schoolhouse, 1 through 5, and attach a sandwich baggie. On the apples, write the addition combinations for 1 through 5. The children shuffle the apples, look at the math fact, and place it in the schoolhouse baggie that has the correct answer.

For *kindergarten,* draw dots on the apples. Have the children count the dots and place the apples in the appropriate Baggies.

For *second grade,* make ten schoolhouses. Write the number combinations for addition and subtraction to 10 or as many apples as you want to use.

September

Instant Math—September

October

Instant Math—October

November

Instant Math—November

December

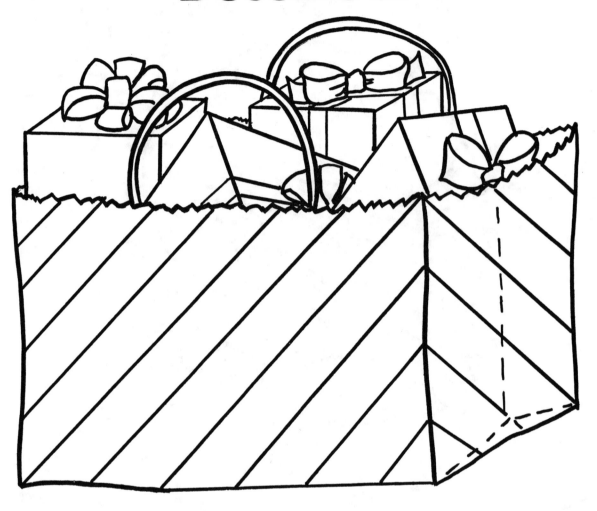

© 1992 by The Center for Applied Research in Education, Inc.

Instant Math—December

January

Instant Math—January

February

Be
Mine

Instant Math—February

March

Instant Math—March

April

Instant Math—April

May/June

Instant Math—May/June